The Myth of Black
Anti-Intellectualism

The Myth of Black Anti-Intellectualism

A True Psychology of African American Students

Kevin O. Cokley

Practical and Applied Psychology
Judy Kuriansky, Series Editor

 PRAEGER

AN IMPRINT OF ABC-CLIO, LLC
Santa Barbara, California • Denver, Colorado • Oxford, England

Library of Congress Cataloging-in-Publication Data

Cokley, Kevin O. (Kevin O'Neal), 1969–
   The myth of Black anti-intellectualism : a true psychology of African American students / Kevin O. Cokley.
      pages cm. — (Practical and applied psychology)
   Includes bibliographical references and index.
   ISBN 978–1–4408–3156–0 (cloth : alk. paper) — ISBN 978–1–4408–3157–7 (ebook)
1. African American students—Psychology. 2. African American students—Race identity.
I. Title.
LC2731.C65   2015
371.829'96073—dc23   2014024157

ISBN: 978–1–4408–3156–0
EISBN: 978–1–4408–3157–7

19 18 17 16 15   2 3 4 5

This book is also available on the World Wide Web as an eBook.
Visit www.abc-clio.com for details.

Praeger
An Imprint of ABC-CLIO, LLC

ABC-CLIO, LLC
130 Cremona Drive, P.O. Box 1911
Santa Barbara, California 93116-1911

This book is printed on acid-free paper ∞

Manufactured in the United States of America

To the ancestors, all of whose names will never be known,
but whose sacrifices made it possible for me to be here ...
and
To Baba Asa Hilliard, who challenged the myth of
Black anti-intellectualism and exemplified the best of
what it means to be African and a Black scholar ...
and
To my students, who have demonstrated that to be young,
gifted, and Black is the norm rather than the exception ...
and
To my parents, Angelo and Elma Cokley, whose support and
pride in me were motivation to always represent them well ...
and
To my children, Asa and Isis, who are blessings from God and
serve as constant reminders of the importance of the work that I do ...
and
To my wife, Germine "Gigi" Awad, whose intellect has pushed
me to be better, and whose love and support made it possible
for me to complete this book.

Contents

Series Foreword

In April 2006, I was invited to attend the third annual Black Counseling Psychologists Conference at Howard University in Washington, D.C. One of the presenters was Kevin Cokley, at the time associate professor of counseling psychology and Black studies at the University of Missouri at Columbia, who spoke on *The Association of Black Psychologists' Response to Hurricane Katrina: Guidelines for Providing Culturally Appropriate Services for People of African Ancestry Exposed to the Trauma of Hurricane Katrina.*

I was impressed by his eloquence and passion in talking about the plight of Black Americans in that devastating disaster. I knew then that this educator had much to say about the definitions and conditions that Black Americans face not only in such tragedies, but also in education and in our present culture. Thus, I was passionate about having this brilliant psychologist write a book about his ideas, reflections, experience, and knowledge. I am thrilled that it has come to fruition in this book, *The Myth of Black Anti-Intellectualism: A True Psychology of African American Students.*

Dr. Cokley's account of his own journey through the school system is riveting. My heart went out to him as the 5-year-old boy who, making the mistake of calling his White teacher "fat," was ridiculed by her for being Black. His later trials through academia, with failing grades and false athletic starts, also brought me to tears.

Cokley's writing reads like a novel. His words draw the reader in, as his strong personality mixed with vulnerability are interwoven with powerful messages and enlightening information about racism and Blackness, backed up by solid research and academic references.

No wonder he has been appointed as editor-in-chief of the *Journal of Black Psychology.* No wonder, too, that he has earned many awards; aptly titled "10 Rising Stars in the Academy" and a "High Flyer." It also makes sense that he was given the Faculty Teaching Award from the John Warfield Center for African and African American Studies at the University of Texas at Austin; and, recently, the University of Texas System Regents' Outstanding Teaching

Award, offered to faculty who have demonstrated extraordinary classroom performance and innovation in undergraduate instruction. His talent comes through in his speaking and writing.

Cokley draws us into his world emerging as a struggling Black student and rising in academia to become a distinguished faculty member. He also draws us into the world of all African American students, making us confront myths about how Black students learn. He enlightens us about terminology—about which my own students and I are often challenged—for Black, African American, race, and ethnicity, noting that Black is a racial term broadly encompassing all people of African descent compared to the more technically ethnic term of African American. This coincides with what I have noticed in my encounters as an NGO representative at the United Nations; that Blacks typically refer to being Black Americans, while others of African descent may prefer referring to their national or cultural heritage—e.g., being Nigerian, Jamaican, or Caribbean.

When I first talked to Kevin about doing a book for my series, I was immediately captivated by the topic about which he had been percolating for years; that of the critique of Blacks as being anti-intellectual. How perfect for us all now to be able to read his thesis about how this is not true, as he sheds light on the complicated interrelationship between Black self-esteem, academic self-concept, and grades, pointing out how behaviors and attitudes are mistakenly interpreted as anti-intellectual.

As the reader is drawn into Cokley's own coming to terms with his racial identity, it is inevitable to confront one's own journey. As a White woman, and also a university educator, I found myself thinking about my own illuminating experiences, including teaching students of varied backgrounds at Columbia University Teachers College, noted for its multiculturalism. My classes about intimacy and relationship are filled with students' captivating reports how their culture from countries all over the world deal with dating, marriage, love, and sex.

Reading Kevin's book brought many experiences to my mind about race and Blackness, as it can for all readers. I recall the disclosure of one UN ambassador I met with while advocating for mental health and well-being to be included in the UN 2015 global agenda. He shared a powerful personal story illustrating how he could relate to the importance of mental health and dispelling stigma. The memory still haunts him, of being a Black man from the islands—the only student of a different color—at a party at a Canadian college he was attending, feeling isolated and pained. Remembering the trauma of that experience made him sympathetic to support the importance of the inclusion of mental health as a global goal, along with poverty, achieving gender equality, and combating diseases.

My racial consciousness has been further heightened as an NGO representative at the United Nations working alongside one of my best friends, Corann

Okorodudu, professor of Psychology and Africana studies at Rowan University. We write advocacy statements together, in which I contribute about the topic about well-being, and Corann contributes about human rights and racial equality.

Racial awareness reached new heights for me, too, when I went to South Africa for the international Congress of Psychology, hosted by my friend Dr. Saths Cooper, an antiapartheid activist who was imprisoned in the same cell-block as Nelson Mandela in the notorious Robben Island prison. I have since penned profiles of Saths, produced a video about his life and ideas, and chronicled his early days as a student activist and now a figure in professional heights as the president of the International Union of Psychological Sciences and cofounder of the Pan African Psychology Union. Writing my *Huffington Post* blog and UPI news commentary about Saths's experiences, spurred by the sad occasion of Mandela's death, taught me much about the intricacies of the apartheid movement and different activism groups, and helped me appreciate even more the stories of Cokley's similar student activism.

In writing this book, Dr. Cokley achieves the goal he values: challenging the idea that Black students are anti-intellectual. He makes psychological and educational social science research riveting for professionals and accessible to the masses. As such, his book should be read by professional, pundits, politicians, parents, clergy, academia, and the public alike, of every race and ethnicity. His book needs to be on the required-reading book list of every education institution.

Cokley provides proof of his thesis that conventional ideas about Black students are not true. One example is particularly illuminating: that the conclusions in the infamous "doll research"—that Black students' preferences for white dolls revealed self-hatred—are faulty. He presents his arguments while engaging the reader with research interwoven with his personal story as well as references to popular culture. He convincingly concludes that Black students are actually very intellectual, inquisitive, and engaged, especially when the curriculum and culturally competent teachers facilitate the students' self-respect that they, their race, ethnicity, and culture, matter and contribute valuably to their community and to civilization.

Dr. Judy Kuriansky
Series Editor, Practical and Applied Psychology

Acknowledgments

This book has been a labor of love. I first started writing it in 2007 and had periodic interruptions that prevented me from writing consistently. My wife, Gigi, has been with me on this journey from the beginning. She encouraged me to pursue my dream of being the author of a book. Without her, undoubtedly the clarity and rigor of my arguments would have been compromised. She gave me time and space when she knew I needed it, and she put up with my singularly minded focus to get the book completed. I also want to acknowledge my children, Asa and Isis, who had to give up valuable daddy time as I spent countless hours working on the book. I will never get that time back, so I hope this book makes some small tangible difference in helping people better understand African American students. I am indebted to the influence of the Association of Black Psychologists (ABPsi). I have literally grown up in ABPsi from being an eager student to now being a professor and editor-in-chief of the *Journal of Black Psychology*. It is from ABPsi that I learned the importance of defending the integrity and humanity of African people. I also want to acknowledge the intellectual influence of Dr. William Cross. My exposure to his work on Black identity as a master's student set the foundation for my research trajectory. He has also served as an exemplar of how Black intellectuals should balance celebrity with humility. Finally, I want to acknowledge the intellectual influence of Baba Dr. Asa Hilliard. As a doctoral student, I would go to his office and drink from the fountain of his wisdom about all things related to African people and Black education. Baba Asa served as an exemplar of how African-centered scholars should passionately defend the humanity of African/Black people without dehumanizing others. There has been no greater intellectual influence in my life.

Introduction: Personal Reflections of an African American Psychologist

ELEMENTARY SCHOOL—THE AWAKENING OF RACIAL AWARENESS

My earliest recollections of school are not all positive. I remember crying on my first day of school when my parents dropped me off. I was five years old, and school was a big and scary place. I did not want to be away from my family. However, my parents assured me that everything would be okay. Once my separation anxiety began to subside, I began to adapt to my new role as a kindergarten student.

I was quickly identified to be a part of a remedial speech therapy program. Developmentally, I was supposedly not speaking at the level of other kids my age. I remember absolutely dreading this program. It was the bane of my young existence (these are obviously adult reflections of a childhood experience)! We would meet for approximately an hour each day in a room isolated from other students. It is noteworthy that a disproportionate number of students required to participate in this program were Black. My mother tells me that this was the case because (White) teachers back then did not think that Black students knew how to speak correctly. My teacher, an older White woman named Mrs. Tucker, was a harsh woman who would lose her patience with me and the other students when we were unable to correctly enunciate certain words. I was embarrassed and ashamed for having to participate in the program, and was obviously self-conscious about the way I spoke. On more than one occasion, I was rendered to tears by her harsh words and treatment of me. Often I was made to feel dumb and inadequate. I choose these words very intentionally to emphasize that I did not feel that way prior to my interactions and experience of this teacher. This experience was largely responsible for my verbal self-consciousness as a child. Fortunately, I had strong, supportive, and active parental involvement in my education, and I really wanted to be perceived as a good student, so I bravely fought to improve my speech and to become a good speaker. My efforts to improve my speaking were also bolstered by my involvement in the Black church, where oral reports of Sunday School lessons were given every Sunday before a supportive congregation. I eventually transitioned out of the speech therapy program when I had demonstrated sufficient improvement in my verbal skills. Several years later, my teachers would recognize me for my excellent reading skills and ability to expressively communicate written material in front of a class.

Like many kids, I was a very active student. I enjoyed school and I loved to learn. My energy and enthusiasm would sometimes get me in trouble, as I was prone to talking a lot and joking around when work needed to be done. I enjoyed playing with my friends and was completely oblivious to issues of race.

That innocence was shattered in an instance after a teacher reprimanded me. Like most children, I did not understand the rules of social etiquette when it comes to making commentary about people's physical appearance. My teacher, Mrs. Riddle, was a very large, dare I say obese, White woman who was known to be a very strict and no-nonsense teacher. One day as I was interacting with some of my classmates, I made a comment about her weight. While my exact words are lost in the recesses of my memory, I do know that I referred to her as fat. She apparently overheard me, and confronted me immediately. She (rightfully so) reprimanded me, telling me that what I said was not a very nice thing to say. She then looked at me squarely in the eyes and asked, "How would you like it if I said something about you being *Black*?"

From the moment those words left her mouth, my entire being was shaken to its core. I had never had any thoughts about anything related to my color. I knew that I looked different from her and the rest of my classmates, but I had never really thought about it. It was strange that given my lack of experience with, and thus lack of consciousness of, racial incidents, I would have been so dramatically affected by her seemingly innocuous comments about my race. There was no obvious anger or emotion behind the question. And yet there I was, on the verge of tears over her comments. Having verbally chastised me, she then escorted me to the sink where I was made to wash my mouth out with soap. In Mrs. Riddle's classroom, when kids uttered words that were considered mean or "dirty," they were punished by washing their mouths out with soap. I guess this act symbolically represented the cleaning of one's mouth of impure words. Whatever the rationale, I felt very badly, and I was not quite sure why. I am sure being called out in front of my fellow students had something to do with my embarrassment. However, in my admittedly at times sketchy and faded memory, I clearly remember Mrs. Riddle's words, and I remember the hot flush of embarrassment that swept over me as the little eyes of my (mostly White) peers stared at me.

When I arrived home, I told my parents of the incident. They were infuriated, particularly with my having to wash my mouth out with soap. Along with my fiery paternal grandmother, they marched to school the next day to confront the principal and Mrs. Riddle about how I was punished. According to my mother, my father expressed his concern about my being used as an example in front of the class. To this day, my mother will not tell me exactly what she said, other than to say that she had a lot to say. My mother was especially appalled about the health implications of such a practice. Under the intense criticism of my family, Mrs. Riddle broke down into tears. She apologized both to my parents and grandmother, as well as to me the next day. I will never know what was in Mrs. Riddle's heart when she made that comment. I am not comfortable characterizing her or the comment itself as racist, but I am also not comfortable saying definitively that she was not racist. What moral lessons could she have hoped to impart on a 5-year-old boy by making that comment? In my estimation, underlying her question was the unspoken belief that there really was something wrong with being Black, something that she could explicitly state if she chose to exercise that option. Perhaps in her mind, her weight and my race carried equivalent negative social stigmas. If she believed this, she was sadly mistaken. Whatever the case, her comment was ill advised, to say the least.

Interestingly, what is most memorable to me about that incident is not what is most memorable to my parents. Their emotional memories were/are tied into the health implications of my punishment, while my emotional memories were/are tied into Mrs. Riddle's comment about my being Black. For my parents, the racial comment, and the disproportionate number of Blacks in the remedial speech therapy program, were just normal reminders about the social and educational status differences that existed between Blacks and Whites in the rural South. For me, these were eye-opening experiences about what it meant to be Black in the educational system. From my earliest recollections of school, if there was any tension between my developing racial identity and academic identity, it was a result of my experiences in school, specifically my interactions with White teachers. It would take years of what psychologists call "corrective emotional experiences" to successfully integrate my racial and academic identities.

MIDDLE SCHOOL—AMBIGUOUS RACIAL SLIGHTS

By my middle school years, I had established myself as a very good student. I was among the top students in my classes, and I had earned the respect of my teachers. I very much enjoyed my teachers, who seemed to genuinely like me. However, these mutual feelings of like and respect changed with my seventh-grade teacher. Mr. Hauser was a White male teacher who taught math. Like many teachers, he also pulled double duty as coach of the boys' and girls' basketball teams. Mr. Hauser was a tough, surly teacher who liked to put students on the spot by solving math questions on the board in front of the class. His pedagogical strategy was to say the number of the assigned math problem, and wait for a student to volunteer to go to the board to solve the problem. The higher the number of the assigned math problem, the more difficult it was. It was apparent that Mr. Hauser liked the really smart kids, as he would call on them often with the expectation that they could answer the tough questions.

While Mr. Hauser's tough, no-nonsense teaching style was effective for helping students learn math, his caustic personality was at times damaging to my confidence in my academic abilities. He seemed to spare few students of his sarcasm, but it was especially pronounced with Black students. He would make off-color jokes that always made me uncomfortable. While I do not remember the specific comments he made, I do remember that I often felt self-conscious about being Black in his presence. He would also make statements that I (and other select students) would end up working in the local factory, thus effectively consigning us to a lifetime of menial labor. We endured this treatment throughout his class. Years later, when I found out that he was subjecting my academically gifted cousin to the same treatment, I wrote him a scathing letter in which I lambasted him for his years of damaging the self-concept of Black students.

HIGH SCHOOL—INTEGRATING AN ACADEMIC AND RACIAL IDENTITY

By high school, I had been identified as a "smart" student, as evidenced by my placement in the highest-level classes that were available. I believed that I was a good student, and fully embraced making good grades as a part of my academic identity. I never considered myself as one of those super-smart, academically gifted students who always made straight As. However, I considered myself an above-average, hard-working student. I made honor roll often, but not all of the time. Consequently, I did not make the National Honor Society, a disappointment that lingered with me for several years.

The defining moment in my young academic career were two programs called Medicine as a Career and Focus on Biology. Medicine as a Career and Focus on Biology were summer enrichment programs geared toward academically gifted minority students (mostly African American) and Appalachian Whites (defined as Whites living in rural Appalachian areas who were presumably economically disadvantaged). The programs brought these students (identified by guidance counselors) together for two and five weeks, respectively, on the campus of Wake Forest University. The purpose of the programs was to encourage more ethnic-minority and economically disadvantaged students to pursue a career in medicine.

I had never been in a setting where there were large numbers of serious, goal-oriented, academically gifted Black students. The pride that I felt from my selection and participation in the programs was immeasurable. This experience was the first explicit experience that connected my identity as a Black student to my academic performance. I can honestly say that it changed me forever. When I completed the summer programs and returned home to get ready for school, I had a renewed sense of purpose. I also had a newfound resentment toward my White classmates, and living in a small, predominantly White "hick" town.

My eyes were now open. I was angry because I felt that for years I had been deprived of the opportunity to reach my potential as a student. I was also angry because I had considered myself a special Black student because I was excelling in my classes. I realized that I harbored beliefs that Black students could not excel academically, and that I believed I was the exception. Living with a group of academically gifted Black students made me realize that I was, paradoxically, special yet not special. A whole new world of possibilities had been opened to me, and my racial and academic identities became more solidified. I had developed a new racial consciousness, and I was now empowered to be more vocal on race-related issues, while other Black students continued to sit back passively. I was ridiculed by certain Black and White students for being too militant, which only fueled my emerging Black consciousness.

COLLEGE—EMERGING BLACK CONSCIOUSNESS AND ACADEMIC STRUGGLES

I achieved somewhat of a milestone by being the first Black student from my high school (and I think from my Pilot Mountain) to get accepted to Wake Forest University. I received the Hankins scholarship, which was a need-based, academic scholarship. Wake Forest University is a small, highly selective private liberal arts school predominated by upper-middle class White students. It was a very proud moment in my life. Within the first couple of days of college, I was approached and asked by some White students if I was a football player. I responded by saying no, and proudly pointed out that I was there on academic scholarship. It was a rude awakening to what would be the first of many "encounters" that the African American psychologist William Cross would describe. I can vividly recall those first few days of college walking in the quad area and seeing a Confederate flag displayed from the dorm room of the Kappa Alpha Order fraternity. That flag was a constant reminder of the history and culture of Wake Forest and the old South, and a reminder that African American students were ethnic and racial minorities in an overwhelmingly White and sometimes unwelcoming environment.

Like many first-year college students, I was overwhelmed with the freedom I had to go anywhere I wanted, stay awake as long as I wanted, and pretty much do anything that I wanted. Academically, I could take whatever classes I wanted. Also like many first-year college students, I was pre-med, and I took biology, chemistry, psychology, and Latin in my first semester. After having attended two summer enrichment camps that were geared toward increasing the number of ethnic minorities in medicine as a career, I was certain that this was my destiny. However, biology and chemistry changed my destiny! I struggled mightily in those classes, and ended up failing both classes while making Cs in my psychology and Latin classes. This was a rude awakening to the beginning of my college experience. I lost my scholarship, and I was immediately placed on academic probation after my first semester. Never had I experienced such academic struggles before. A wave of self-doubt suddenly surrounded me, and my academic self-concept had been shaken to its core. Had I bitten off more than I could chew? Was I not smart enough to be there? Did I really belong? If I flunked out of school, it would embarrass not only me, but my family. My parents were extremely proud that I was attending Wake Forest University. Black students from Pilot Mountain were not supposed to be academic achievers. We were not supposed to go to colleges like Wake Forest University. If I flunked out, I would be confirming the doubts of all the naysayers who (I and my family believed) wanted me to fail.

The atrocious start in my first year haunted me for my entire four years of college. As conventional wisdom goes, it is much easier to lower your grades significantly than it is to raise them significantly. The truth of the matter was that I really was not as academically prepared as I should have been to do well in college. I did not know how to study effectively, nor did I know the amount of time that was needed to thoroughly master the information being presented in classes. I did not understand the importance of scheduling regular meetings with my professors to discuss material that I did not understand. For that matter, I did not even always know what I truly understood and what I did not. I rarely sought academic help, and when I did, I could not help but feel self-conscious about being a Black student that needed academic assistance. My academic self-concept took a beating during those four years of college, and left me wondering what my future held in store.

During the time that my academic self-concept was taking a beating, my racial consciousness and Black identity was growing. I entered Wake Forest already having a pretty strong Black identity that had been enhanced by my experiences in the two summer enrichment programs at Wake Forest. However, college is an experience in which racial and ethnic differences are often emphasized to a degree not seen in high school. There are numerous student organizations based on racial and ethnic identities and themes. Additionally, famous and provocative speakers are routinely brought to campus to stimulate and foster dialogue on important racial issues. I immediately became involved in the Black Student Association (BSA), a staple organization seen on many predominantly White college campuses. I also joined the Gospel Choir and later a Black fraternity. The BSA was the center of social and political activity for Black students on campus. One of my most vivid memories of the BSA was protesting South African apartheid. The BSA had partnered with another organization to stage a dramatic enactment of apartheid activity in the student cafeteria. When given a sign, several Black males (myself included) walked to several seemingly unsuspecting White females (who were actually willing participants in the demonstration), grabbed them out of their seats and dragged them away. The reaction was swift and dramatic. Several white males stood up, clearly angered and disturbed by what they were witnessing, and demanded that we stop. At this point, a member of the BSA stood in front of the cafeteria and made a statement about apartheid, indicating that what people had just witnessed was a regular occurrence to Black people living under the brutal regime of South African apartheid. The adrenaline rush that I received from participating in this demonstration was incredible. More importantly, it was an influential experience that contributed greatly to my emerging critical racial consciousness.

Two speakers were brought on campus that perhaps had the greatest influence on my critical racial consciousness and increasing pride in my racial identity during college. These speakers were Jawanza Kunjufu and Na'im Akbar. Jawanza Kunjufu is best known for his books entitled *Countering the Conspiracy to Destroy Black Boys*. Na'im Akbar is a highly regarded and outspoken Black psychologist who advocates an Afrocentric philosophy to understand the conditions and psychology of Black folks. The impact that hearing these two men speak had on my racial identity was incredible. Both men exuded a confidence, racial pride, and sense of purpose and commitment to Black people that I had never witnessed before. Na'im Akbar (or Baba Na'im, as he is affectionately called) was especially influential, as he sowed the early seeds of what would become my embrace of Afrocentric psychology.

Years later, I attended my 20-year class reunion. I was excited to see friends and acquaintances whom I had not seen in many years. One of these individuals was a White female named Tina. Tina had attended high school with me, and we ran track together both at East Surry High School and for a summer track club. We were also in all of the same advanced classes, and played in the band together. We were close friends in and out of school. Our lives were remarkably parallel in academics and athletics, so it was no surprise that we both applied and were accepted to Wake Forest University. Interestingly, I received a need-based academic scholarship while Tina received a track scholarship. I lost my opportunity to receive a track scholarship anywhere once I false-started at the North Carolina State Track Championships. Nevertheless, the Wake Forest head track coach invited me to be a member of the track team as a walk-on (non-scholarship athlete). I gladly accepted the invitation.

An interesting thing happened during my time at Wake Forest University. Once Tina and I started college, our paths rarely crossed outside of track. We were not in the same student organizations, and we did not socialize together. We had never talked about this, and in fact we had very few conversations while attending Wake Forest. So 20 years later, I contacted Tina via Facebook and arranged to meet with her at our 20-year class reunion. During dinner, we reminisced about old times, especially the traumatic false start that I had in high school. Then, a conversation that I did not anticipate took place. Tina indicated that something had been bothering her for so many years, and she had always wanted to talk with me about it. She basically wanted to know what happened to us. Why didn't we stay close while in college? I thought about her question very carefully. I do not think I had ever really thought about it much, and as I was reflecting on her question, the answer became obvious. I decided to be very candid with her, and responded by saying that I essentially discovered my Blackness in college. I lapsed into a mini-lecture on the psychosocial development of Black college students, and how my racial identity was impacted by attending a predominantly White school. I talked about the importance of being around other students similar to myself, and the importance of belonging to Black student organizations for my racial identity. I also talked about my academic struggles, and the fear of failure that I thought would be attributed to being Black.

By the time I was a senior, I did not know what my future held in store for me. I did not think my grades were good enough to get accepted into any graduate program in psychology, so I never considered that a viable option. I participated in the job fair and hoped that my resume would be attractive to some company. I was encouraged when a pharmaceutical company contacted me for an initial interview. Later, I received another invitation for a second interview. I was very excited, and thought that I might actually have the chance of having a job waiting for me upon graduation. However, a third interview did not happen, and a job offer never materialized. I was in a very bad place emotionally. In an independent research paper that I wrote in my last semester, my words reflected an angry and disillusioned Black male student, as evidenced by the title of my paper, "The Unknown Societal Conspiracy to Denigrate African-American Males." In the paper I made the following statement: "My feelings about myself are such that I feel as though I have disappointed my family, teachers, and, most importantly, myself. I did not make Dean's List once while in college. My feelings of high aspirations upon entering college have been shattered beyond repair. My future is unknown. The person that I thought I would be upon graduation has never materialized. Many would say that I made my bed, now I must lie in it. And to a certain degree, this is true. However, I refuse to accept all of the blame. Social forces at work all around me have molded me into an embittered young Black man. Now I'm almost a college graduate. God only knows what young, uneducated and impoverished Black men must be feeling."

As I reflect on my college years, I see that my time at Wake Forest was marked by two distinct experiences: one of academic struggle, and one of emerging Black consciousness. It is no accident that these themes would later define much of my scholarly work on African American students.

GRADUATE SCHOOL—BLACK IDENTITY AND ACADEMIC EXCELLENCE

Through an act of serendipity, a fraternity brother from the University of North Carolina at Chapel Hill happened to be on Wake Forest's campus.

After introducing ourselves, he told me that he was going to a master's program in counselor education at the University of North Carolina at Greensboro (UNC-G). I had never heard of counselor education, but I became very interested as he described the different tracks. I was particularly interested in the student development in higher education track. For some reason, I thought that I might have a decent chance of getting accepted into a program. I applied to two master's programs and was accepted into one (Appalachian State University) and provisionally accepted into the other (UNC-G). Given that UNC-G was closer and the number-one ranked program in the country, I chose to go there.

I was very excited and nervous about starting graduate school. Being provisionally accepted meant that I needed to obtain at least a 3.5 GPA in my first year, a GPA that I never obtained in college. However, I found that my graduate classes were much more interesting, and I was very motivated to do well. Consequently, I maintained well above the 3.5 minimum GPA. My original career goal was to be a director of minority affairs because of the influence of Dr. Ernie Wade, who held this title at Wake Forest University. However, my goal changed after taking a Multicultural Counseling class. I was captivated after reading work by Derald Wing Sue, William Cross, Janet Helms, and Thomas Parham, particularly by how boldly they addressed issues of race, racism, and racial identity. I noted that most of them were counseling psychologists, so I made the decision to pursue a doctorate in counseling psychology.

I applied for and was accepted into several doctoral programs. I chose Georgia State University because it was in Atlanta (considered a Black mecca), and because of the presence of several Black professors, including Dr. Asa Hilliard. Dr. Hilliard was a prominent Afrocentric psychologist and Egyptologist who was best known for his work on issues related to Black education. Dr. Hilliard (or Baba Asa, as he was often called) was a passionate and tireless proponent for the unlimited intellectual and academic potential of Black students. He also believed strongly in the role that African/Black culture should play in the education of Black students. His influence, combined with my involvement in the Association of Black Psychologists, gave me an intellectual and activist grounding that became the lens through which I approached all of my academic work. Consequently, I excelled in graduate school.

COLLEGE PROFESSOR—RESEARCH AND TEACHING AS AUTOBIOGRAPHY

From the moment that I started my doctoral program, I knew that I wanted to be a college professor. It was a dream that I knew would not be easy to fulfill, but one that I was committed to pursuing. I applied to several positions and eventually was invited to interview at Southern Illinois University at Carbondale (SIUC).

SIUC had a large number of African American students from Chicago, and the counseling psychology doctoral program had a proud history of graduating African American students. The counseling psychology program also had a history of producing or hiring some of the biggest names in counseling psychology, especially multicultural psychology (e.g., Janet Helms, Robert Carter, Thomas Parham, Frederick Leong, Laura Brown).

My job talk was competent, but certainly not extraordinary. I was 28 years old, and I had only one publication. There were other candidates with much stronger applications. For various reasons, these candidates did not work out. However, I was still fortunate enough to receive a job offer, which I happily accepted. Later, it was communicated to me that the faculty thought I would be a good teacher with potential to grow into becoming a solid researcher. They took a risk on me, and for that I will always be grateful.

I have been a college professor for 16 years, and have taught at three universities: Southern Illinois University at Carbondale (SIUC) (6 years), the University of Missouri at Columbia (3 years), and currently at the University of Texas at Austin (7 years). My research and teaching largely reflect my experiences as a Black male negotiating the challenges of being in predominantly White academic environments. My experiences are also reflective of the experiences of thousands of Black students at every level of education. From the moment that I decided to be a college professor, I knew that I wanted to teach classes related to race and culture. As a graduate student, I envisioned myself teaching a class on African American psychology as well as a class on the psychology of race and racism. When I started at SIUC, there was a course listed in the Black Studies curriculum entitled "The Black Personality." Given the opportunity to teach an African American psychology course, I was asked to teach this particular course. My first decision was to change the name of the course to "Psychology of the African American Experience," based on my belief that the title "The Black Personality" was much too reductionistic and essentialist to accurately capture my philosophy and approach in teaching the class.

Teaching this class has been without a doubt the most fulfilling aspect of being a professor. I have seen a level of enthusiasm, motivation, and achievement from African American students that energizes me and serves as a reminder about why I became a professor. Every institution where I have taught has been the same experience. The class is a powerful and transformative experience and makes it hard to believe that African American students have problems with academic motivation. Yet, in spite of my years of experience teaching this class, and witnessing its educational and psychological impact on African American students, there still exists the widespread belief that African American students do not possess the motivation to excel in school. This sentiment is probably best exemplified in the book *Losing the Race: Self-Sabotage in Black America*, authored by the linguistic scholar John McWhorter. This book places the blame for

African American student underachievement squarely on Black American culture, making an argument that anti-intellectualism is rampant throughout Black American culture while minimizing the roles of structural and institutional factors and their impact on the motivational psychology of African American students. This book prompted me to write the article "What Do We Know about the Academic Motivation of African American College Students? Challenging the Anti-Intellectual Myth," published in the *Harvard Educational Review*. That article, combined with previous and subsequent articles and editorials on the academic woes of African American students, ultimately led me to write this book.

Note: Throughout this book I use the terms Black and African American interchangeably. I recognize that the term Black is a racial term and broader in scope than African American, which is more properly thought of as an ethnic term. I also recognize that the term Black technically encompasses all people of African descent. However, in this book, when I use the term Black, I am typically referring to the Black American experience of individuals whose ancestors were enslaved. I do this primarily because in everyday discourse, Black is typically used to refer to Black Americans, while other individuals of African descent typically prefer to be identified by their national or cultural heritage (e.g., Nigerian American, Jamaican American, African, Caribbean, etc.). Of course, issues of identity are not so easily categorized in this manner, as I discuss in the next chapter.

1

Who Am I? The Search for Black Identity

WHAT'S IN A NAME: AFRICAN, AFRICAN AMERICAN, OR BLACK?

In the 1991 film *Boyz N the Hood*, a scene from a school in inner-city Los Angeles is shown where one of the main characters, 10-year-old Tre Styles, is sitting in a classroom listening to a rote, uninspired lecture about the history of Thanksgiving. When the teacher asks the class the name of the early English settlers, the class says in unison "Pilgrims"; however, Tre shouts out "Penguins," which results in laughter from the class. After asking Tre why he always has something funny to say, the teacher asks him if he would like to teach the class. Tre surprises the teacher by saying yes, and steps in front of the class. After pointing to a picture of Africa on the map and asking the class to identify it, the following exchange takes place:

> Tre: "Did you know that Africa is where the body of the first man was found? My daddy says that's where all people originated from. That means everybody's really from Africa. Everybody. All y'all. Everybody."
> Male Student: "I ain't from Africa. I'm from Crenshaw Mafia!" [Class laughs.]
> Tre: "Like it or not, you from Africa."
> Male Student: "I ain't from Africa. You from Africa. You African booty-scratcher!"

This short but poignant exchange is symbolic of the tensions that exist in the African American community around identity, specifically as it relates to Africa. *Over 20 years later when I am teaching my Psychology of the African American Experience class, I show the film* Black Is Black Ain't *where the phrase "African booty-scratcher" is used once by the narrator. Invariably there will be chuckles from some of my African American students, while most of my African students sit in silence, disappointment, and anger. When I confront my students about the problematic nature of that phrase and ask why they laugh, the typical response is something along the lines of it sounding funny. They assure me that it is not racial and has nothing to do with Africans or stereotypes of Africans. When I ask if they have heard of comparable phrases such as "Asian booty-scratcher" or "Hispanic/Latino booty-scratcher," the students say no, and I can see the epiphany slowly spread as they are confronted with the uncomfortable truth of how they have been socialized to view Africa and Africans as primitive and savage.*

As an African American psychologist, I have dedicated much of my career to understanding the importance of identity. It pains me that this dehumanization of, and disconnection from, Africans is still prevalent among some African Americans. To drive home my point about some of the specific identity challenges of African Americans, I use the example of how Asian Americans and Mexican Americans are sometimes referred to in shorthand as simply Asians and Mexicans. This is especially the case with Asian American students, who are often referred to simply as Asian students. While it may sometimes be an annoyance for these students, there is not typically righteous indignation around being identified solely with the continent or country of their cultural heritage. However, try referring to African American students as Africans, and watch the acrimony that ensues.

A prevailing theme in the history of African Americans involves tensions surrounding identity. These tensions include both the minimization and/or outright denial of an African cultural heritage, and ultimately represent the struggle for agency and self-determination in naming and defining ourselves. No other group of people has the history of multiple name changes as African Americans. Africans were enslaved and forcibly removed from mostly central and West Africa. It is widely believed and taught that the first Africans arrived in North America as indentured servants and were brought to Jamestown, Virginia, in 1619. Interestingly, recent scholarship indicates that the first Africans arrived in North America as free men more than a century before the landing of the Mayflower at Plymouth Rock (Restall, 2000). The teaching of this important history has not yet become a part of standard curriculum.

Nevertheless, what remains true is that Africans came to the Americas from many ethnic groups, including the Akan, Gbe, Yoruba, Igbo, and Kongo (Lovejoy, 2005). They hailed mostly from the coastal regions of Africa such as Angola, Congo, Ghana, Guinea, Nigeria, and Sierra Leone as well as West Central Africa. The identity of being an African was not a salient moniker for Africans brought to the Americas as indentured servants and enslaved individuals, because their most salient identity was their ethnic affiliation. However, once brought together under the system of chattel slavery, their common bond of being African eventually became more salient than their ethnic group affiliations. This became apparent through the names of the institutions they created, including the African Episcopal Church, the African Masonic Lodge, the First African Baptist Church, the African Free School, the Children of Africa, and the Sons of Africa (Holloway, 1990).

An additional factor that influenced the expression and embracing of African identity was the role of European slave owners, who constantly worried that Africans who were empowered would be less likely to be subservient and more likely to be rebellious. Africans who were strongly identified with their African cultures and ethnic groups were ultimately seen as threats to the status quo; thus, the goal of European slave owners was to completely break the will and spirits of the enslaved Africans. This is powerfully captured in a scene from Alex Haley's *Roots*, where Kunta Kinte is whipped by another enslaved African acting as a headman and under the direction of the European slave master. He was asked repeatedly by the slave master, "What's your name?" to which he would respond "Kunta Kinte." Finally, after numerous lashes, a physically and spiritually broken Kunta finally responded by saying "Toby," the name forced upon him by his slave master.

This history of different ethnic group affiliations, coming from different African countries and regions, attempting to forge a unified African identity, and being forced to deny African culture and adopt the name given by the oppressor, has all contributed to the confusion and constant search for names, labels, and ultimately identity among people of African descent in the United States.

DEFINING RACIAL AND ETHNIC IDENTITY

Living in a highly racialized society, especially as a racial/ethnic minority, makes you acutely aware of your identity when you are in a predominantly White environment. For many racial/ethnic minorities, the minority experience becomes a central part of their identity. *I once had a conversation with a White female colleague where she wanted to have a real honest discussion about race. After seeking assurances from her about really wanting to "go there," I stated the disclaimer that once that door was open, there was no closing it. I proceeded to tell her that not a day goes by where I was not reminded that I was a Black man in a predominantly White department. She found that hard to believe, and was somewhat incredulous that that was really my experience. Of course, this was hard for her to understand and relate to, because it was such a foreign experience to her. Her reality was that she did not live her life constantly thinking about her race because being White was the normative experience for her. In my Multicultural Counseling class, I ask my White students what it is like to be White. Without fail, they all struggle to answer the question. When you ask a racial/ethnic minority what it is like to be "Black," "African American," "Hispanic," "Latino," "Asian," "Asian American," "Native American," or "Arab American," they can usually answer the question without batting an eye. That is because their experiences as a racial/ethnic minority are often central aspects of their identity.*

The concept of identity refers to how individuals come to define themselves. Identity reflects how individuals choose to self-identify as well as how identities are ascribed to individuals by society. The question "Who Am I?" strikes at the heart of identity concerns and succinctly captures a common human concern. Informed by social identity theory, the psychologist William Cross stated that identity consists of personal identity and reference group orientation (Cross, 1991). Personal identity refers to the attitudes and feelings an individual has about oneself; specifically, how individuals perceive themselves (self-concept) and how individuals feel about themselves (self-esteem). Reference group orientation refers to the attitudes and feelings individuals have toward their racial and ethnic group (or some other social group to which they belong). The general understanding of race involves the belief that humans belong to biologically discrete categories that share similar physical characteristics including skin color, facial features, hair texture, and other hereditary traits. Most social scientists agree that race is socially constructed and not a biological reality; however, the belief in the "truth" of race has real social and psychological consequences, one of which is the identity that results from the belief in race.

Racial identity refers to the collective identity that is constructed by any group of people socialized to view themselves as part of a racial group (Helms & Cook, 1999). All individuals in the United States have been socialized to view themselves racially. Perhaps the best example of this can be seen with the census, where individuals must identify with one or more racial classifications. Racial identity is less about the actual racial classifications, and more about the meaning and emotions attached to the racial classifications. Given the racialized history of the United States, racial identity is especially salient for racial minorities who are part of groups that have historically experienced prejudice and discrimination. For many individuals, the most salient part of their identity is related to their ethnicity and cultural heritage more than being part of a racially marginalized and oppressed minority. Ethnic identity refers to the subjective sense of having membership in an ethnic group that involves (1) how individuals label themselves ethnically, (2) a sense of belonging to the ethnic group, (3) how positively (or negatively) individuals evaluate the ethnic group, (4) the amount of knowledge one has about the ethnic group, and (5) the level of involvement one has in ethnic group activities (Phinney, 1990, 1996).

In many ways, racial identity and ethnic identity are similar concepts that have been used interchangeably. Indeed, one might argue that similar to racial identity, ethnic identity is also a collective identity constructed by any group of people socialized to view themselves as part of an ethnic group. Likewise, one might argue that similar to ethnic identity, racial identity refers to a subjective sense of membership in a racial group that involves self-labeling, sense of belonging, positive or negative evaluation of the racial group, amount of knowledge of racial group, and the level of involvement in racial group activities. While the terms are similar and overlap to a certain degree, I believe it is useful to maintain a conceptual distinction between them, especially for purposes related to academic outcomes. At the heart of racial identity is the idea that individuals are born into groups that are stratified into racial hierarchies. Everyone socialized in a racialized society knows that racial hierarchies exist, and everyone knows their place within these hierarchies. Racial identity is largely formed as a consequence of internalizing beliefs about race in a highly racialized society. On the other hand, at the heart of ethnic identity is the idea that individuals are born into groups with rich histories and cultural heritages as well as distinctive cultural traits. Ethnic identity is largely shaped by the messages received from family, school, and society about one's ethnic group.

MODELS OF RACIAL AND ETHNIC IDENTITY

Nigrescence: A Psychology of Black Liberation

Psychologists have long been interested in issues of identity among African Americans, and specifically the development of racial and ethnic identity. In the area of African American psychology, racial identity remains one of the most researched and overall popular topics for scholars (Cokley, 2002b, 2005; Cokley & Chapman, 2009). As a result, several models have been developed to better understand the role of identity in various psychosocial outcomes. No model has been more influential than William Cross's model of psychological Nigrescence. During the late 1960s and early 1970s, William Cross was a graduate student in the psychology department at Princeton University. Cross witnessed the tremendous social upheaval occurring during the Civil Rights and Black Power Movements. Through the use of interviews, phenomenological data, and his own interactions with Black individuals who were undergoing changes, Cross developed a model that seemed to capture the psychological changes in the consciousness of Blacks as a result of their involvement in the social unrest and political movements. He characterized these changes as the "Negro-to-Black Conversion Experience" and described the changes as occurring in a series of stages (Cross, 1971).

Pre-Encounter

During the first stage, Pre-Encounter, the individual was socialized to hold what Cross characterized as anti-Black, non-Black, or the opposite of Black views. These individuals were not involved in any of the political movements. Individuals in the Pre-Encounter stage held negative and/or stereotypical views about Blacks, and they romanticized Whites. In short, individuals were essentially pro-White and anti-Black in their worldview.

Encounter

During the second stage, Encounter, the individual experienced an event or interaction that challenged her or his previous Pre-Encounter worldview. For many African Americans, the assassination of Martin Luther King Jr. in 1968 was their encounter. This was especially the case for individuals who had not been politically active in the Civil Rights or Black Power Movements. For some individuals, an encounter experience occurred while observing or experiencing some form of discrimination. For other individuals, an encounter could simply be a conversation with someone who embraced their Blackness and who was conscious and politically active.

Immersion-Emersion

Whatever the exact nature of the encounter, the individual was propelled into what Cross called the Immersion-Emersion stage. Having experienced an encounter, individuals in the Immersion-Emersion stage became immersed in a stage of psychological Blackness. These individuals now passionately embraced their Blackness, and all things Black. They became involved in Black organizations and were in many ways more demonstrably Black in their clothes and hairstyles. In other words, they embraced a Black aesthetic. This newfound love of all things Black, or pro-Blackness, was also coupled with a hatred or disdain of all things White. While this stage was a predictable and necessary stage of identity development for Black people, Cross viewed it as a problem when individuals stagnated here. In other words, Cross did not believe that it was ultimately the most optimal state of being for Black folks to base their pro-Blackness on hatred of White people. He viewed that as actually being inadequate for Black liberation. It was also an emotionally exhausting state of mind to be in.

Internalization

Consequently, some individuals began to emerge out of this intense emotional and reactive state of Blackness into what Cross called the Internalization stage. Individuals in the Internalization stage achieved an inner security and peace with their Blackness and maintained a strong Black identity. They continued to be committed to a pro-Black worldview; however, their Blackness was no longer coupled with hatred or disdain toward White people. Importantly, however, these individuals did not commit themselves behaviorally to a plan of action. They recognized the racism and discrimination against Black people and abhorred it; however, in many ways, they intellectualized the experience of being Black with no tangible plan on challenging or confronting the institutions responsible for their oppression.

Internalization-Commitment

Finally, there were a small number of individuals who reached a level of self-actualization for which activism became a part of their Black identity. These individuals become committed to a plan of action that would result in the betterment of the conditions of Black people. Cross described the individual as moving beyond rhetoric and into action. Individuals in this stage were sympathetic toward other Blacks who were still stagnated in the Immersion-Emersion stage, because they recognized the importance of that stage in their own psychological development. These individuals were committed to helping other Blacks move from what Cross called "reactionary White hatred" to a more healthy expression of Black pride that also involved the acquisition of Black skills coupled with compassion and Black humanism. Cross used Malcolm X as an example of someone who had reached the stage of Internalization-Commitment, yet still recognized the importance of his Immersion-Emersion experience as a member of the Nation of Islam.

While the original Nigrescence model is cited most frequently and what Cross is best known for, in actuality the model was modified and expanded considerably (Cross, 1991; Cross & Vandiver, 2001) as Cross and his colleagues responded to conceptual and theoretical critiques of the model along with methodological and psychometric critiques of its measurement (e.g., Helms & Parham, 1996). Recognizing that the Pre-Encounter stage was overly simplistic and did not fully capture the range of attitudes that could represent this stage, Cross theorized that Pre-Encounter attitudes were further differentiated into Self-Hatred, Miseducation, and Assimilation. Self-Hatred included intensely negative feelings of self-loathing related to being Black. Miseducation included the internalization and acceptance of negative stereotypes about Black people. Assimilation attitudes de-emphasized race or Blackness and instead emphasized the importance of assimilating into mainstream American society. Similarly, Cross believed that Immersion-Emersion attitudes could be further differentiated into pro-Black attitudes and anti-White attitudes. Cross made this distinction because he believed that individuals could be passionately pro-Black without necessarily having anti-White attitudes. He believed that the anti-White attitudes could be separated from the pro-Black attitudes, even while the actual measurement of this has not been entirely successful. Finally, Cross, theorized that Internalization attitudes could be further differentiated into Biculturalism, Multiculturalism, and Afrocentricity. The Biculturalism attitudes emphasized an identification with race and one other group, such as gender or being an American. The Multiculturalism attitudes emphasized an identification across multiple social identity groups, including race, sexual identity, gender, etc. The Afrocentricity attitudes emphasized an identification with Afrocentric values and beliefs.

Cross originally linked racial identity attitudes that might be seen as more "advanced" or "developed" in Nigresence (i.e., later "stages") to more optimal outcomes related to mental health. More recently, Cross has argued that there are different pathways to optimal mental health for Black people, such that assimilationist attitudes are equally as likely to result in good mental health as multiculturalist or Afrocentric attitudes. The only exception would be that individuals who harbor self-hating racial identity attitudes are typically not going to have optimal mental health.

Black Identity Reconceptualized: The Multidimensional Model of Racial Identity

Cross's Nigrescence model has been the most popular model of Black identity in the literature and has greatly influenced the work of other scholars (e.g., Carter, 1995; Cokley, 2002b, 2005; Helms, 1990; Helms & Parham, 1996; Parham, 1989; Parham & Helms, 1981). The model's apparent developmental thrust had a lot of appeal to mental health professionals, who used it to conceptualize notions of a "healthy" Black identity. However, not all scholars agreed with the idea of a model prescribing a healthy or unhealthy Black identity.

Robert Sellers and his colleagues developed the Multidimensional Model of Racial Identity (MMRI) (Sellers, Smith, Shelton, Rowley, & Chavous, 1998). Rooted in theories of social identity (Stryker & Serpe, 1982, 1994), the MMRI recognizes that social identities have stable properties but are also influenced by situations. In other words, there are certain attitudes about being Black that are likely to be relatively stable across situations, but there are certain situations that are likely to make being Black more salient. Importantly, however, the MMRI is a model of Black identity that does not assign, implicitly or explicitly, any evaluative labels to Black identity. Instead, Black identity is theorized to have multiple dimensions that are not hierarchically ordered in terms of "good" or "optimal."

Two important questions are at the core of the MRRI. First, how important is race in the individual's perception of self? This is an important question because it is often assumed that race is always a salient and important identity for African Americans. Rather than making it a foregone conclusion, this becomes an empirical question to be asked and tested under the MMRI. The second question at the core of the MMRI is, what does it mean to be a member of this racial group? Again, Sellers and his colleagues did not want to assume that they automatically know what it means to be Black for every Black person. Instead, they believe that it is an important question to be asked and tested under the MMRI.

The MMRI consists of four dimensions, which include racial salience, racial centrality, racial regard, and racial ideology. *Racial salience* refers to how relevant race is to one's self-concept in a particular moment or situation. For most African Americans, even those for whom being Black is not a particularly important part of how they define themselves, being the only Black person at a Ku Klux Klan rally, being the target of a racist joke, or being called the n-word would make being Black very salient.

One story that I sometimes share with my students is about the time when I was in a faculty meeting as a young, untenured professor. We were doing student evaluations, and we had spent quite a bit of time discussing one of my advisees. This student was a Black male who had been having a number of difficulties academically and in his clinical training. After much discussion, the training director stated that if he did not get his act together, his "Black ass" would be kicked out of the program. I will never forget that moment. I looked around the room at my colleagues and no one would make eye contact with me. To this day, race has never been any more salient for me as a professor than at that moment. After the meeting, I left without speaking to anyone and went across campus to the Black Studies Department to talk about what had happened. Predictably, they were upset and asked me how I responded. I indicated that I was so shocked that I did not say anything. My colleagues indicated that I could not let the incident go unaddressed, and that I had to confront the individual. The next day I went to my colleague's office to express my feelings, and she apologized profusely. She went on to apologize again in front of the faculty. Not only had race been made a salient part of my identity during that incident, I also began to question my own racial identity. I speculated that there must have been something about me and my self-presentation that made it okay for that type of comment to be made. I vowed to never again come across in such a way that would make it seem okay to make such a blatant racial comment.

The next dimension, *racial centrality*, refers to how often being Black is an important part of an individual's self-concept. In the story that I shared about my White female colleague, I communicated to her that I think about being Black every day of my life. When you are constantly reminded that you are a Black person in a predominantly White world, being Black is likely going to be an important part of your identity. Clearly, being high in racial centrality was disconcerting to her. The next dimension, *racial regard*, refers to an individual's evaluative judgment about being Black. Racial regard consists of *public regard*, which is how much an individual feels the public holds positive or negative views about being Black, and *private regard*, which is how an individual feels about being Black and about other Blacks. The last dimension, *racial ideology*, refers to an individual's beliefs about how a Black person should act. Historically, there have been primarily four types of racial ideology that have existed in the African American community: nationalist philosophy, oppressed minority philosophy, assimilation philosophy, and humanist philosophy. Individuals with a nationalist philosophy believe in self-determination, the uniqueness of the Black experience, and are more likely to participate in Black organizations. Individuals with an oppressed minority philosophy believe in the similarities between Blacks and other oppressed minorities. Individuals with an assimilationist philosophy believe that like other groups, Blacks should work within the system to effect change. Individuals with a humanist philosophy believe that all humans share a similarity that is greater than their race, gender, class, or other social identity.

While the four racial ideologies are presented as separate and exclusive, in fact they are not mutually exclusive. However, individuals are likely to embrace certain racial ideologies more than others. For example, Rev. Jeremiah Wright, the pastor emeritus of President Obama's former church, Trinity United Church of Christ, would be characterized as espousing a Black nationalist racial ideology. In fact, it was this brand of racial ideology that led Republicans and conservatives to have serious concerns about the racial ideology of President Obama. To be president of the United States, President Obama has needed to articulate an assimilationist and humanist ideology that de-emphasizes issues of race and racial identity. Whether this reflects his true beliefs or is a matter of political expediency is a topic for speculation and debate. The NAACP is a civil rights organization dedicated to fighting for social justice for all Americans. Its philosophy reflects more of an oppressed minority racial ideology. Individuals who are activists and have a more progressive politics are most likely going to subscribe to an oppressed minority and/or nationalist ideology, while individuals who de-emphasize group identity and group differences are more likely to subscribe to an assimilationist and/or humanist ideology.

ETHNIC IDENTITY

In the late 1980s, Rev. Jesse Jackson along with other prominent leaders advocated for the use of the term African American. The argument made was that the term Black was a racial term that referred only to skin color, and it did not connect people to their cultural and ethnic identity that was rooted in Africa. While many Blacks embraced the label African American, there were still some who were ambivalent about the term, and others who were outright hostile toward it. Other ethnic groups have also struggled with names and self-definition. However, it cannot be ignored that other ethnic groups such as Mexican Americans, Cuban Americans, Irish Americans, Chinese Americans, and Japanese Americans have names that reflect a connection to a specific geographical area, history, and culture. A shift to ethnicity and ethnic identity would ideally help foster greater pride and self-esteem in one's group.

In the early to mid-1990s, developmental psychologist Jean Phinney began writing about the increasing importance of ethnicity in the United States. Phinney conceptualized ethnicity and race as largely overlapping constructs. She argues for the use of ethnicity because of the problems associated with the construct of race. She made a seminal contribution to the literature by identifying three psychological aspects of ethnicity: *culture*, *identity*, and *minority status* (Phinney, 1996). Ethnicity as culture refers to the norms, values, attitudes, and behaviors that are embraced by an ethnic group. Defining and describing African American culture has not always been an easy task. This is largely because the history of African Americans reflects many cultural influences, including multiple African ethnic groups, European Americans, and Native Americans. Along these lines, some scholars have minimized the influence of any retentions of African cultures in contemporary African American culture, arguing instead that African American culture primarily reflects a syncretism of Old World and New World cultures (Mintz & Price, 1992). Regardless of one's position in this debate, most people would agree that African American culture exhibits certain distinctive characteristics, which the father of Black psychology, Joseph White, has identified as cultural strengths. These cultural strengths include improvisation, resilience, connectedness to others, spirituality, emotional vitality, gallows humor, and a healthy suspicion of White folks.

Ethnicity as identity refers to how strongly an individual identifies with her or his ethnic group. There is a certain politics that goes with strength of ethnic identity. In the African American community, individuals who are perceived as not having a strong ethnic identity and being more White identified are sometimes derisively referred to as "orioles." Interestingly, there appears to be a phenomenon among ethnic minority groups of referring to in-group members with perceived weak ethnic identities as some sort of food. Mexican Americans with perceived weak ethnic identities are derisively referred to as "coconuts," Asian Americans as "bananas," and American Indians as "apples." All of these terms refer to individuals who are perceived as "selling out"—that is, being "black," "brown," "yellow," and "red" on the outside but "white" on the inside. The message here is simple: one should be proud of their ethnicity and have a healthy and positive ethnic identity. If one does not (or is perceived as not) having a strong ethnic identity, their ethnic group will treat them accordingly.

Ethnicity as minority status refers to the experiences of ethnic groups of color who have a history of being discriminated against, marginalized, and underrepresented. The term ethnic minority largely reflects the idea that ethnic groups who are numerical minorities are more likely to have experienced a history of discrimination and underrepresentation. For African Americans, our status as minorities in virtually every sector of society (with the exception of sports and entertainment) is well documented. It is this dimension of ethnicity that appears to be most directly linked to poorer outcomes in education, health, and socioeconomic status (among other domains). It has been suggested that it is this dimension of ethnicity more than culture and identity that causes individuals to seek out individuals who are similar to them. Better understanding this phenomenon was the driving force behind Beverly Tatum's bestselling book *Why Are All the Black Kids Sitting Together in the Cafeteria?* (Tatum, 1997). In reality, one could also argue that all three dimensions are equally important in decisions to be around other members from one's ethnic group.

AFRICAN-CENTERED/AFROCENTRIC IDENTITY

"We're Not Americans, we're Africans who happen to be in America. We were kidnapped and brought here against our will."

—Malcolm X

"If a cat has kittens in an oven, does that make them biscuits?"
—Malcolm X

The quotes above by Malcolm X represent a counter ideology to the Civil Rights Movement and the related American Black identity movement. The first quote was made in Malcolm's "Ballet or Bullet" 1964 speech made in Washington Heights, New York. The second quote was made in Chicago as Malcolm was debating a Black leader about the merits of Blacks calling themselves Americans. Malcolm believed that Blacks should reject the term American because this is a White man's country. Both quotes reflect Malcolm's disdain of a country whose history includes forcibly removing Africans from Africa and bringing them to the United States to enslave, rename, and oppress them. Malcolm thought it made no sense for Black people to identify as Americans given this history, and given that Black people were still experiencing institutional discrimination. For Malcolm and many other Black leaders and intellectuals, the rightful identity for Black people in America was to see themselves first and foremost as African people. The driving ideology was related to the previously discussed argument made by Jesse Jackson regarding the name African American. However, unlike Jackson's argument, proponents of a more African-centered ideology de-emphasize the American side of Black people's identity, instead choosing to see identity as Malcolm demonstrated with his kitten-biscuit metaphor. That is, for Black people, America is simply the destination where Africans were taken. This counter ideology is a specific variation of Black nationalism that has been referred to as Afrocentricity. The term Afrocentricity (sometimes referred to as Afrocentrism) was used as early as the 1960s by Kwame Nkrumah and also in the early 1970s, but it was popularized by the African American scholar Molefi Kete Asante (1980). Afrocentricity refers to a perspective in which African people are agents placed at the center of all analyses. The term African is used diasporically; that is, it refers not only to Africans on the continent of Africa, but also to all people of African descent who moved to other places throughout the world. From this perspective, African Americans, Afro-Caribbeans, Afro-Brazilians, and Afro-Asians, among others, would all be seen as essentially Africans living in different geographical locations. As an intellectual movement, Afrocentricity has generated much scholarship (Asante, 1990, 1998; Gray, 2001; Hamlet, 1998; Ransby, 2000; Ziegler, 1995), and is viewed by some scholars as the preferred paradigm of the discipline of Black studies (Asante, 2006; Azibo, 1992; Conyers, 2004; Karenga, 2002; Mazama, 2001; Semmes, 1981). However, it has also generated much criticism (Howe, 1998; Lefkowitz, 1996; Peters, 1994, 2001). The major criticisms of Afrocentricity include: (a) it distorts and/or fabricates history for the purpose of raising Black self-esteem, (b) it is based on poor scholarship, (c) it essentializes the identity of people of African descent into a falsely homogenous cultural group (i.e., it views all people of African descent as sharing similar cultural traits and a common African essence), and (d) it promotes homophobia. These criticisms of certain strands or expressions of Afrocentricity are undoubtedly valid; however, I believe the criticisms are more reflective of individual scholars' interpretation of Afrocentricity than the tenets of the paradigm itself. For example, there is nothing hegemonic or inherently oppressive about the idea that people of African descent should center themselves in their own cultural reality to better understand the world in which they live. This is the true essence of the Afrocentric paradigm.

> To Be African or Not to Be? That is truly the Fundamental Question!
> —Asa Hilliard

According to a story shared by the renowned African-centered psychologist Dr. Wade Nobles at the annual convention of the Association of Black Psychologists, the quote above by the African-centered psychologist and Egyptologist Dr. Hilliard was a serendipitous utterance that cleverly and succinctly captured the core beliefs of African-centered psychologists. That is, people of African descent are either going to consciously choose to be African, or they will, existentially speaking, cease to exist. The quote from Dr. Hilliard, affectionately referred to as "Baba Asa" in African-centered circles, inspired a group of essays by African-centered scholars that examined the theme "To Be African" (Kwadwo, 2000). To quote from Dr. Nobles, "The essential issue to note . . . is that neither time, circumstance, conditions of cruelty and oppression, nor adopted legal status, change us from being African . . . We are Africans whose birth place locates us in America" (Nobles, 2000, p. 23).

It should come as no surprise that Black psychologists have been among the strongest proponents of an Afrocentric paradigm. Afrocentric psychologists have long argued that people of African descent cannot be fully understood (or understand themselves) without taking into account their African cultural heritage. These scholars see the issue of embracing our African identity as the most important issue facing all people of African descent. Each scholar focuses on different aspects of the Afrocentric paradigm, but the common thread in all of their work is embracing the truth of our African identity. For example, Dr. Kobi Kambon and Dr. Linda James Myers focus on the importance of worldview (Kambon, 1998, 2004; Myers, 1988). Dr. Na'im Akbar is one of the original founders of the approach labeled African psychology. Throughout his career he has focused on the mental liberation of African Americans (Akbar, 1996, 1998). In his books and articles, he writes in a highly accessible way to reach as many people as possible, emphasizing the importance of self-knowledge and of embracing an African identity. Dr. Wade Nobles is considered to be the preeminent theoretical scientist in African psychology. His work has focused on Black family development (Nobles, 1985), African philosophy (Nobles, 1972), and African psychology and spirituality (Nobles, 1986). As a counseling psychologist who has focused on racial identity, Dr. Thomas Parham has perhaps done the best job of integrating Black racial identity with an African identity (Parham, 1997; Parham, Ajamu, & White, 2010). However, in his more recent scholarship he has emphasized the importance of an African ethnic identity over a Black racial identity (Parham, 2002).

INFLUENCE OF NEGATIVE IMAGES AND MESSAGES ON BLACK IDENTITY

As reviewed in this chapter, there have been many different ideas expressed about being Black. Consequently, individuals have held a range of beliefs and attitudes about the meaning and importance of being Black. I focus on this theme of Black identity because of the constant barrage of negative messages that have been communicated about Black people. This is not to say that there are not positive images and messages communicated about Black people. One needs to look no further than President Barack Obama as an example. However, it is also true that President Obama has been the recipient of some of the most vile and racist rhetoric ever experienced by a president. A search of the Internet reveals numerous depictions of President Obama as a monkey or a terrorist, and the birther movement is considered by many to be motivated by thinly veiled, deep-seated racism. In essence, this communicates to Black people that even if you have a Harvard degree and become the president of the United States, at the end of the day, you are not immune from racism. I believe this inundation of negative images and messages about Black people has contributed to the creation of an African American psychology and Black identity that shares elements with other oppressed groups but also has unique characteristics due to the specific history of African Americans.

In my Psychology of the African American Experience class, I show the educational video *Free Your Mind, Return to the Source African Origins* by Dr. Asa Hilliard. Near the beginning of the video is a segment called "The Defamation of African People." Dr. Hilliard starts off with this segment to establish a historical context for the negative themes related to people of African descent. He provides several powerful examples to make his point. The first example is an article from the 1910 *Encyclopedia Britannica* about the Negro. A quote from the article stated that "Mentally the Negro is inferior to the White." The article went on to state that as Black children get older, they become dumber while White children become smarter. The second example was a page out of the Johnson catalog advertising "Nigger Make-Up" for White people to perform Blackface. The third example was a product sold by Colgate in the Far East around 1986 called "Darkie Toothpaste." The toothpaste included a picture of what appears to be a Black person on the front with the exaggeration of Black facial features. The fourth example included a postcard showing a Black man and a possum in a tree entitled "A Coon Trees a Possum." The fifth example was an advertisement for soap with a picture of a Black face in the middle of a watermelon; such depictions were especially prominent between the 1920s and 1960s. The sixth example was a textbook used in the late 1800s in the United States entitled "Ten Little Niggers." Dr. Hilliard argues that all of the images, and countless more, were designed to defame Black people.

Turning to the media, Dr. Hilliard discusses the idea that there is a formula for most Black television shows and that in most instances, the writers of Black television shows up to the 1980s were White. Using examples from *The Jeffersons*, *Sanford and Son*, and the character J. J. from *Good Times*, Dr. Hilliard argues that these shows essentially depict Black people the way White people see Black people, which in most instances was as stereotypes and caricatures. More recent examples can be seen in reality shows such as *Flavor of Love* and *I Love New York*, where the main characters perpetuated images of Black people as buffoons, materialistic, hypersexual, hyperaggressive, and prone to violence. It is significant that over 6 million viewers watched the finale of the first season of *Flavor of Love* (Giannino & Campbell, 2012).

Other examples of more subtle negative messages can be found in discussions of affirmative action. In the recent Supreme Court case of *Fisher v. The University of Texas*, the plaintiff, Abigail Fisher, argued that she was denied admission because she is White. While the debate on how to increase diversity and achieve a critical mass of ethnic minority students has been ongoing, it is without question that the focus tends to be on African American students. The uncomfortable topic of race is omnipresent every year during admissions time. I have witnessed it firsthand as a member of admissions committees, and during faculty discussions of applicants' qualifications. The concerns are usually about the lower academic qualifications of Black students. These concerns are sometimes discussed openly among the faculty, and other times more furtively behind closed doors. In some instances, the message is directly or indirectly communicated to White students that minority students have it easier and receive preferential treatment. This message is then communicated to Black students. *I remember vividly a conversation I had in my first year of the doctoral program with a White male student. We were getting to know each other and trying to form a bond in our cohort. At some point in the conversation he shared with me his fears about not getting accepted into the doctoral program because he is a White male. He communicated that he believed it would not be as difficult for minority students to get accepted as it was for him as a White male. As upset as I was from his innuendo, I gave him credit for being honest enough to say how he really felt. Nevertheless, this brief conversation served as a catalyst for my motivation. In retrospect, I can see how it contributed to the edge that I had as a Black graduate student, and wanting to prove that I belonged.*

More recently was an issue in my current program where many students of color (and some White students) were unhappy about the culture of the program, especially regarding issues of safety and multiculturalism. After an accreditation site visit, the program received critical feedback regarding the culture of the program. As a result, the faculty created a survey for the students to receive anonymous feedback about their feelings and experiences. Among the many disturbing comments was one in particular that I will never forget. A student reported that a faculty member had made the following comments to her: "Students of color are unfair recipients of special privileges and their comments about culture bias reflect knee-jerk reactions, intellectual laziness, and a refusal to learn required material."

It is not hard to imagine that a faculty member who believes this harbors biases and prejudices toward Black students, which would be manifested in their evaluations of these students. These incidents reflect what Derald Wing Sue has referred to as racial microaggressions. Racial microaggressions are daily, common verbal, behavioral, and environmental slights and indignities that are directed toward Blacks and other racial minorities (Sue, Capodilupo, & Holder, 2008; Sue, Nadal, Capodilupo, Lin, Torino, & Rivera, 2008).

What is the cumulative effect of these racial microaggressions on the collective identity and psychology of Black students? Additionally, how resilient must Black students be to maintain a positive and healthy Black identity in the face of these unrelenting negative images and messages?

BLACK IDENTITY AND THE MYTH OF BLACK ANTI-INTELLECTUALISM

This chapter lays the foundation for the rest of the topics covered in this book. Black identity is a theme that is directly or indirectly implicated in discussions of Black achievement. This book critically interrogates the idea that an anti-intellectual Black identity is primarily responsible for the academic underachievement of Black students.

Writing this book presents a number of intellectual challenges and philosophical tensions for me. First, I agree with Richard Valencia and am very critical of what he has called the "deficit thinking" paradigm that seems to dominate discussions around ethnic minority student achievement. I am a strong believer in the critical roles that institutional, economic, and social factors play in educational outcomes of African American students. There is indisputable evidence that teacher biases, prejudice, and racial discrimination in schools adversely affect achievement outcomes of African American students. There is also indisputable evidence that socioeconomic status is an important factor in the so-called achievement gap that exists between African American students and White and Asian students.

As a psychologist, I have been trained to focus on individual differences to account for differential educational outcomes. In other words, I have been trained to focus on variables such as academic motivation, resilience, self-esteem, self-concept, and racial/ethnic identity as explanatory factors of African American student achievement and supposed anti-intellectualism. However, my colleagues in certain social science disciplines (e.g., anthropology and sociology) are critical of psychologists for what they see as a failure to sufficiently theorize and account for the role of systemic and institutional factors related to racism. They see a focus on the individual as absolving the roles of societal and institutional oppression. I am very sensitive to this critique, and to a certain point I agree with them. However, where I differ with them is around the issue of individual agency. How do you explain the fact that two individuals of equal ability, raised in the same household and exposed to the same environmental circumstances of racism, discrimination, and oppression, can have dramatically different educational and academic outcomes? As a psychologist, I am especially interested in being able to answer this question. To the extent that the environment can be changed to make it more optimal for African American students to achieve, I strongly support that. However, I think it is also equally important to better understand why some Black students are able to be academically successful in racist environments and challenging circumstances, while other Black students are unsuccessful. In my mind, it is not an either/or proposition, but rather a both/and proposition. Both approaches are necessary, and in fact I believe that both inform each other. If Black identity plays any significant role, I want to better understand what that role is. However, in doing so, I want to be careful not to "blame the victim," which is another criticism that can be leveled by those who focus on individual factors. Thus, as a scholar, I find myself walking on an ideological tightrope between focusing on the individual factors that contribute to academic achievement and perceptions of Black anti-intellectualism, and focusing on institutional factors that undoubtedly play an equally important role. The truth of the matter is that you cannot (or you should not) talk about one without talking about the other.

In the next chapter, I discuss the literature linking the racial and ethnic identity of Black students to their academic achievement. As is true of much research in this area, the conclusions are somewhat equivocal. Nevertheless, I hope to be able to glean some kernels of truth that can be useful for scholars, teachers, counselors, and parents as they try to better understand how Black identity is implicated in academic achievement.

2

Racial/Ethnic Identity and Academic Achievement: Is This the Right Paradigm to Explain the Achievement Gap?

The 2007 film *The Great Debaters* was the story about how a debate team from a small historically Black institution in Texas, Wiley College, was able to compete in the national debate championship against Harvard University and win. Set in 1935, the film depicted the harsh reality of Jim Crow laws and racial prejudices of the time. In one scene, the professor and debate coach Melvin Tolson (played by Denzel Washington), is preparing the Wiley College debate team and he makes the following statement: "Denigrate. There's a word for you. From the Latin word *niger*, to defame, to blacken. It's always there, isn't it? Even in the dictionary. Even in the speech of a Negro professor. Somehow, *black* is always equated with failure."

Being Black in this country has always been associated with inferiority, especially intellectual and academic inferiority. While it is now considered impolitic to explicitly link the words Black and inferior in mainstream dialogue about academic achievement, other buzzwords and catchphrases are used that essentially communicate the same message. No other buzzword or catchphrase better symbolizes this link between being Black and assumed to be intellectually inferior than the *achievement gap*. The achievement gap is defined by the National Education Association as "the differences between the test scores of minority and/or low-income students and the test scores of their White and Asian peers." The meaning of achievement gap has moved beyond standardized test scores to also include grades and other academic outcomes such as graduation rates.

The questions that are often asked (either publicly or privately) go something like this: Why do Black students perform poorer academically compared to White and Asian students? What is it about being Black that is so consistently linked to academic underachievement? Some observers attribute the achievement gap to innate biological and genetic differences in intelligence (e.g., Herrnstein & Murray, 1994; Jensen, 1973; Rushton, 1997; Rushton & Jensen, 2005). Rather than focus on psychological, social, or even cultural explanations underlying race and racial identity, this hereditarian approach focuses on the presumed biology of race and racial identity. Interestingly, there appears to be virtually no scientifically agreed-upon identification of biological or genetic markers that serve as definitive mechanisms which "cause" Black students to perform poorer than White and Asian students. The hereditarian position posits that the achievement gap is attributable to 50% genetic influences and 50% environmental influences (Rushton & Jensen, 2005). However, a review of hereditarian research and scholarship suggests that much more than 50% attention is placed on the role of genetic influences. Like most reputable social scientists, I categorically reject any notion that Black academic underachievement is linked to biological and genetic differences in intelligence.

A second explanation focuses more on the psychological aspects related to Black identity. The basic question asked is, "What is the relationship between Black identity (racial or ethnic) and academic achievement?" The commonly held assumption is that there is something about the racial and ethnic identity of Black students that is inimical to academic achievement. This question has been the focus of countless dissertations, research studies, and commentaries. However, like many topics in academia, there is more disagreement than agreement on the exact nature of the relationship. Some researchers and scholars have found that the racial or ethnic identity of African American students is negatively related to academic achievement (e.g., Cokley, McClain, Jones, & Johnson, 2011; Fordham & Ogbu, 1986; Harper & Tuckman, 2006; McWhorter, 2000; Worrell, 2007). Other researchers and scholars have found that the racial or ethnic identity of African American students is or can be positively related to academic achievement and outcomes (Chavous et al., 2003; Cokley & Moore, 2007; Oyserman, Kemmelmeier, Fryberg, Brosh, & Hart-Johnson, 2003; Sellers, Chavous, & Cooke, 1998; Spencer, Noll, Stoltzfus, & Harpalani, 2001). Still other researchers have found no relationship between racial or ethnic identity and academic achievement (Awad, 2007), a minimal positive relationship (Lockett & Harrell, 2003), or an indirect positive relationship (Cokley & Chapman, 2008).

It is no wonder that comments and observations made about Black identity and academic achievement are so divergent given that the research literature is wildly inconsistent. People clearly have their opinions about Black students, and have their opinions about how Black identity helps or harms academic achievement. As a researcher, I believe it is important to try to make sense of this equivocal literature in order to provide useful information that informs educators, administrators, and anyone who works directly with Black students and/or is concerned about the academic achievement of African American students. In the following sections, I will briefly review the evidence for (a) the negative influence of racial and ethnic identity on academic achievement, (b) the positive influence of racial and ethnic identity on academic achievement on academic achievement, (c) no influence of racial and ethnic identity on academic achievement, and (d) mixed/conditional influence of racial and ethnic identity on academic achievement. I will then conclude by offering a synthesized analysis of this literature.

NEGATIVE INFLUENCE OF RACIAL AND ETHNIC IDENTITY

In John Singleton's 1995 movie *Higher Learning*, a scene is shown where a Black female college student, Monet, is called a "Black bitch" by a White male. This occurs during an exchange on the phone as Monet is trying to protect her White female roommate who has been raped. Incensed, Monet goes to the room of Fudge, a pro-Black, Afrocentric, 6-year senior and apparent self-appointed source of Black consciousness for Black students. Fudge leads a group of Black males to the White fraternity house and, after identifying the White male who verbally disrespected Monet, drags him out of the fraternity house and makes him say the following: "I apologize, beautiful Black woman, mother of the earth, queen of the universe." Fudge can be considered the classic case of a Black student (usually male) who has a heightened sense of Black identity and Black consciousness; however, this does not necessarily translate into doing well in school. In fact, Fudge believes that school is a game that he has already mastered. He prides himself on not assimilating. At one point when students start to leave for class, he says "Y'all some trained Negros. As soon as you hear a bell you go running."

During my undergraduate years at Wake Forest University, I was an active member of the Black Student Alliance (BSA). The BSA was a politically active organization, and during that time period, South African apartheid was still in effect. The BSA was upset that Wake Forest had not divested from companies who had business dealings with apartheid South Africa. To protest Wake Forest's failure to divest, the BSA planned a demonstration in the cafeteria. Along with some White student allies, the plan was to have certain members of the BSA go to "random" White students eating and to forcefully pull them out of their seats and drag them out of the cafeteria. This was to demonstrate the political reality of Black South African citizens. I was completely enthralled by these types of Black-consciousness political activities. My Black consciousness was growing by leaps and bounds; however, my burgeoning Black consciousness did not translate into making better grades. This is a phenomenon that I've seen over the years with some Black students, especially Black male students. While I did not disidentify with the importance of academics, I certainly struggled with reconciling my increased Black identity and consciousness with my academic struggles.

This disparity in Black consciousness and academic performance was revealed in Ralph Johnson's (1993) dissertation entitled "Factors in the Academic Success of African American College Males." He found that African American male students who were deemed to be successful (GPA > 2.5) had significantly lower African self-consciousness (Mean = 206.40) than African American male students who were deemed to be academically unsuccessful (GPA < 2.0) (Mean = 223.02). Johnson concluded that a strong African self-consciousness or Black identity was incongruent with the educational system.

It is important to more closely examine the published empirical studies that have found a negative relationship between racial or ethnic identity and academic achievement. A closer examination may reveal some insights about why a negative relationship was found. Below I review a representative sample of some of these studies, including some of the more highly cited studies in this area. These studies have generally been conducted with high school or college students.

High School Students

Witherspoon, Speight, and Thomas (1997) conducted a study with 86 African American high school students involved in an Upward Bound program at two predominantly White universities in the Midwest. There were 56 females and 30 males. Racial identity was measured using the shortened form of the *Racial Identity Attitude Scale* (RIAS) (Parham & Helms, 1981). The RIAS includes four subscales that coincide with Cross's Nigrescence theory: *Pre-Encounter, Encounter, Immersion/Emersion,* and *Internalization.*

Males reported significantly higher Immersion scores and lower GPAs than females. The authors found a negative correlation between Encounter scores and GPA as well as Immersion scores and GPA. Additional statistical analyses indicated that only Immersion scores negatively predicted GPA. Interestingly, the authors characterize their findings as demonstrating high school students with both (1) positive Black identity attitudes and good grades, and (2) pro-Black/anti-White attitudes and poor grades, in spite of the fact that there were only statistically significant negative correlations reported. The authors conclude that there were within-group differences among African American high school students regarding the ways that racial identity attitudes related to academic achievement.

In another quantitative study, Harper and Tuckman (2006) surveyed 289 African American high school students from three public high schools in a large, midwestern school district. The authors did not identify a breakdown of the sample by sex. The authors used a shortened version of the *Multidimensional Inventory of Black Identity* (Sellers, Rowley, Chavous, Shelton, & Smith, 1997) that included *Racial Centrality, Private Regard,* and *Public Regard* subscales. Academic achievement was measured by school-reported grades as verified by the high school guidance counselors.

The authors were able to statistically determine Black racial identity profiles of freshmen and seniors. The profiles included: *Idealized,* who were students who had high levels of racial centrality, public regard, and private regard relative to the mean scores; *Buffering/Defensive*, who were students who had low levels of public regard and high levels of racial centrality and private regard relative to the mean scores; *Alienated*, who were students who had low levels of racial centrality, public regard, and private regard relative to the mean scores; and *Low Connectedness/High Affinity*, who were students who had high levels of private regard and low levels of both racial centrality and pubic regard.

Results indicated that among both freshmen and seniors, *Alienated* students had statistically higher grade point averages than *Idealized* students. Among the reasons offered by the authors to explain this finding (which was counter to their expectations) included the possibility that Alienated students may identify more with the White majority and may be disassociating from Black students they perceive negatively. Unfortunately, the authors did not offer clear reasons why the *Idealized* students would have lower grade point averages.

Worrell (2007) conducted a quantitative study involving 319 ethnically diverse high school students attending a summer program for academically talented students. The students consisted of 28 African Americans, 28 Hispanics, 171 Asian Americans, and 92 Whites. The overall sample consisted of 57.7% females; however, the breakdown of sex by ethnicity was not provided. The *Multigroup Ethnic Identity Measure* (MEIM) (Phinney, 1992) was used to measure ethnic identity. The MEIM includes two subscales that measure ethnic identity attitudes (i.e., ethnic behaviors, affirmation and belonging, and achievement) and other group orientation attitudes (willingness to interact with and learn about other ethnic groups). Academic achievement was measured via self-reported GPA by the students.

Worrell found that ethnic identity only significantly predicted GPA for African American students. Specifically, he found that ethnic identity was a statistically significant negative predictor, while other group orientation was a statistically significant positive predictor. Worrell concluded that the data support previous research and theorizing that African American students who were strongly identified with their ethnic group could develop an oppositional stance toward schools and the majority culture.

In a quantitative study, Cokley, McClain, Jones, and Johnson (2011) surveyed 96 African American students from an urban public high school in Houston, Texas. The sample consisted of 41 males and 55 females. Racial identity was measured using the *Racial Centrality* subscale (Sellers et al., 1997). Academic achievement was measured by school-reported grades as verified by the homeroom/English teacher. The results indicated that racial identity was a statistically significant negative predictor of GPA. The authors conclude that African American adolescents who have narrow conceptions of Blackness and racial stereotypes about what it means to be Black are at greater risk for lower academic achievement.

POSITIVE INFLUENCE OF RACIAL AND ETHNIC IDENTITY

Interestingly, it is much more difficult to find examples in popular culture of Black identity being explicitly and positively linked to academic achievement. No Black-themed movie that I reviewed explicitly addressed how being Black was consistent with high academic achievement. For example, the movie *Lean on Me* was set in an underperforming inner-city high school where Black, Latino/a and White students were all struggling academically. While the principal, Joe Clark, had high expectations for all the students, he never explicitly discussed how academic excellence and being Black are interconnected.

The movie *Higher Learning* follows the lives of an African American track star who struggles with academics (Malik Williams), along with a White male who is socially awkward and out of place and a White female who is very naïve and shy. While the movie showed Malik's growing Black consciousness, there were no explicit messages that linked Black consciousness with academic excellence. The primary message learned by Malik was to challenge and question Eurocentric education (even calling his Black professor an Uncle Tom) rather than mastering the education and then using it to advance his interests (i.e., the interests of Black people). This is the distinction Mwalimu Shujaa (2003) makes between education and schooling. Schooling essentially perpetuates and maintains the status quo for domestication, while education is the transmission of beliefs, values, and sensibilities that result in being able to determine what is in your interests, and in being able to distinguish your interests from the interests of others. While Malik appeared to move through the stages of Cross's Nigrescence model of racial identity, his identity as a Black man was never fully integrated with his identity as a student. In fact, his primary motivation for doing well in school appeared to have more to do with maintaining his track scholarship and eligibility than with being a Black man who should strive for academic excellence.

The movies *The Great Debaters* and *Akeela and the Bee* both showcased Black students who excelled in debating and spelling. In the case of *The Great Debaters*, there was clearly a racialized historic context, while race was never an issue explicitly brought up in *Akeela and the Bee*. Neither movie explicitly connected the students' Black identity to their academic accomplishments. Being consciously and proudly Black is never part of the narrative involving academic achievement in movie depictions of African American students. It is no wonder that conventional wisdom suggests that an emphasis on academic achievement is not part of Black culture. Depictions of African American student achievement in the movies seem to be more comfortably made when there is no obvious link to a strong racial identity.

It is only in the world of documentaries that you see attempts to link Black identity to academic achievement. The 2011 documentary *Black Lights* highlights the failure of many Chicago schools in promoting high academic achievement among African American students. However, unlike the usual narrative of Black student failure and the disconnect between being consciously Black and being a strong student, *Black Lights* showcases African American students with strong Black identities. This is exemplified by one student saying, "I am a Black Light because I always strive for success." A recent CNN documentary on the achievement gap highlighted an African American male star athlete, Jawan Minor, who, like a few other African American students, was doing well in school. He was head of the Minority Achievement Committee, otherwise known as the MAC scholars. The MAC scholars are high-achieving seniors who mentor younger students. The messages about being Black and also being a high academic achiever were an important part of the documentary, even while the explicit linking of Black identity and academic achievement was more subtle.

It is against this backdrop that we review several empirical studies that found a positive relationship between racial or ethnic identity and academic achievement. A closer examination may reveal some insights about why a positive relationship was found. These studies have generally been conducted with middle school students and high school students.

Middle School Students

Oyserman, Bybee, and Terry (2003) conducted a longitudinal quantitative study involving 132 middle school African American students participating in an after-school enrichment program. The sample included 64 males and 68 females. Academic achievement was measured via students' self-reporting of their grades based on a 9-point scale (0 = mostly Fs; 1 = mostly Ds and Fs; 2 = mostly Ds; 3 = mostly Cs and Ds; 4 = mostly Cs; 5 = mostly Cs and Bs; 6 = mostly Bs; 7 = mostly As and Bs; 8 = mostly As). Racial identity was initially measured using a large sheet of paper divided into two large blocks labeled "me" and "not me." Students placed stickers with self-descriptors on the block that best described them as an African American. The self-descriptors represented the three dimensions of what the authors called "racial/ethnic identity" (REI): *Connectedness* (e.g., "member of my church"), *Achievement* (e.g., "work hard in school"), and *Awareness of Racism* (e.g., "stared at"). In a follow-up study, REI was measured by three items representing each of the three dimensions: *Connectedness* ("I feel close to others in my community"), *Awareness of Racism* ("Some people might have negative ideas about my abilities because I am Black"), and *Embedded Achievement* ("It is important for my family and community that I succeed in school"). The authors found that spring grades were predicted by significant interactions with gender; specifically, REI connectedness for boys and REI-embedded achievement for girls. The authors conclude that aspects of REI can promote more concern about school.

Yasui, Dorham, and Dishion (2004) conducted a quantitative study with a community sample of 159 successful and high-risk middle school adolescents. The sample included 82 African Americans and 77 European Americans, of which there were 92 females and 67 males. Students were considered successful if they had a GPA above 2.0, had no discipline issues, and had not failed a class. High risk was determined by use of the *Teacher Risk Scoring Index* (Soberman, 1994). Academic achievement was measured by grades for academic subjects obtained from school-based assessment measures. GPA was reported on a 4-point scale ranging from 1 (D or lower) to 4 (A- to A). Ethnic identity was measured by the *Multigroup Ethnic Identity Measure* (Phinney, 1992). Two subcomponents of ethnic identity were specifically examined: (a) affirmation and sense of belonging, and (b) ethnic identity achievement.

Ethnic identity was significantly and positively correlated with GPA for the African American adolescents. Additionally, lower levels of ethnic identity were highly associated with being identified as at risk, which, the authors suggested, indicates the importance of ethnic identity as a predictor of negative adjustment for African American adolescents. The authors conclude that ethnic identity is most important for ethnic minority youth who are in socioeconomically disadvantaged contexts.

Altschul, Oyserman, and Bybee (2006) conducted a quantitative longitudinal study involving 98 African American students and 41 Latino students from three low-income, urban Detroit schools. Data on the sex of the participants were not included. Academic achievement was measured via grade records obtained from the school or district. Racial/ethnic identity (REI) was measured by four items representing each of the three dimensions: *Connectedness* ("I feel part of the Black community"), *Awareness of Racism* ("Because I am Black, others may have negative expectations of me"), and *Embedded Achievement* ("It is important for my family and the Black community that I succeed in school").

The authors found that grades and REI changed linearly over time, such that at each time point in data collection, students who were high in REI Awareness of Racism had higher GPAs. Additionally, youth who were higher in both REI Connectedness and REI Embedded Achievement had higher GPAs. The authors conclude that there is a positive influence of REI content on academic outcomes.

High School Students

Taylor, Casten, Flickinger, Roberts, and Fulmore (1994) conducted a quantitative study with a sample of 344 African American and White students attending public and Catholic high schools in a large northeastern city. There were 135 public school African American adolescents, 60 Catholic school African American adolescents, and 100 Catholic school White adolescents. The discrepancy in numbers was due to the researchers using the students' self-description of their ethnicity rather than the school's description. For the entire sample, there were 69 males and 95 females from the public high school, and 89 males and 91 females from the Catholic school. Academic achievement was measured using the students' grades taken from their school records in three classes: English, math, and social studies. Ethnic identity was measured using the *Ethnic Identity Development* subscale of the *Multigroup Ethnic Identity Measure* (MEIM) (Phinney, 1990).

The authors found that for the public school African American students, ethnic identity was positively correlated with GPA, and, when placed in a larger model of variables, also significantly predicted GPA and engagement in school. These findings were not replicated with the Catholic school African American or White students. The authors speculate that the expression of racial or ethnic identity in the Catholic setting may be discouraged compared to the public school setting. The authors conclude that more research is needed to understand the mechanisms through which ethnic identity impacts school performance and engagement.

MINIMAL OR NO INFLUENCE OF RACIAL AND ETHNIC IDENTITY

High School Students

Chavous et al. (2003) conducted a longitudinal quantitative study involving 606 African American adolescents. The sample included 287 males and 319 females. The students were obtained from four public high schools (80% African American) in the Midwest (presumably Michigan, given the location of the authors). Students with GPAs of less than 3.0 were selected for the study. Academic achievement was obtained from school district records. Racial identity was measured using the *Multidimensional Inventory of Black Identity* (Sellers et al., 1997) that included *Racial Centrality*, *Private Regard*, and *Public Regard* subscales.

A preliminary analysis found that students out of school had lower racial centrality and private regard than students still in school. The authors did not find any of the racial identity variables to be significantly correlated with 12th-grade GPA. The authors were able to statistically identify four racial identity profiles. The first profile was identified as *Buffering/Defensive*, which was characterized as students having positive group affiliation that was self-protective in light of having an awareness of racism. The second profile was identified as *Low Connectedness/High Affinity*, which was characterized as students having low race centrality, high private regard, and low public regard. These first two profiles both have positive beliefs about being Black, but race was not a significant part of their overall identity. The third profile was *Idealized*, which was characterized by students having higher-than-average scores across all three racial identity dimensions. The fourth profile was *Alienated*, which was characterized by students having lower-than-average scores across all three racial identity dimensions. The authors also did not find any significant differences in GPA between the four racial identity profiles. The authors speculated that the failure to find relationships between racial identity and GPA was related to the developmental period of the students examined. Interestingly, the authors characterize the Buffering/Defensive group as having the highest academic achievement and attainment, but this appears to be based on having the highest percentage of students in school rather than on GPA.

College Students

Lockett and Harrell (2003) conducted a quantitative study with a sample of 128 African American students attending a historically Black university (HBU). The authors reported that 79% of the sample was female, which translates to about 101 females and 27 males. Academic achievement was measured via students' self-reported GPA. Racial identity was measured using the *Racial Identity Attitude Scale* (RIAS) (Helms & Parham, 1990). The RIAS consists of four subscales: *Pre-Encounter, Encounter, Immersion,* and *Internalization.*

The authors found that only Internalization attitudes were significantly predictive of GPA. However, additional analyses also indicated that the racial identity and GPA link was significantly reduced once self-esteem was taken into account. In other words, the unique effect of racial identity via internalization attitudes on GPA was lessened because of the impact of self-esteem. The authors conclude that the unique effect of racial identity on academic achievement is minimal, and that research in this area has been characterized by overinterpretation of the data.

Awad (2007) conducted a quantitative study with a sample of 313 African American college students. The first sample was used to predict GPA and consisted of 168 African American students. The second sample was used to predict Graduate Record Examination scores (GRE), consisted of 145 African American students, and included 32 men and 113 women. Academic achievement was measured via students' self-reported GPA, and a GRE verbal section was used. Racial identity was measured using the *Cross Racial Identity Scale* (CRIS) (Vandiver, Cross, Worrell, & Fhagen-Smith, 2002). The CRIS is based on the revised version of Cross's Nigrescence theory (Cross & Vandiver, 2001) and contains five subscales: *Pre-Encounter Assimilation, Pre-Encounter Miseducation, Pre-Encounter Self-Hatred, Immersion-Emersion, Internalization Afrocentricity,* and *Internalization Multiculturalist.*

Awad found that none of the racial identity subscales were correlated with GPA or GRE scores. The racial identity subscales also were not predictive of GPA or GRE scores. She concluded that other variables such as academic self-concept are more pertinent variables to predicting GPA than racial identity, which she suggested may be indirectly related to GPA by influencing variables like academic self-concept.

MIXED/CONDITIONAL INFLUENCE OF RACIAL AND ETHNIC IDENTITY

Middle School Students

Gordon, Iwamoto, Ward, Potts, and Boyd (2009) conducted a quantitative study with 61 Black male middle school students, of which 29 students were involved in an eighth-grade mentoring program intervention. Thirty-two students did not receive the intervention. The program focused on racial identity development, academic identification, and academic performance for Black male students enrolled in a single-sex cluster. Academic achievement was measured via GPAs and standardized achievement test scores that were obtained from school records. Racial identity was measured using the *Racial Identity Attitude Scale* (RIAS) (Helms & Parham, 1996). The RIAS consists of four subscales: *Pre-Encounter, Encounter, Immersion,* and *Internalization.*

The authors found that Internalization attitudes were positively predictive of GPA. Internalization attitudes were also positively predictive of the Connecticut Mastery Test (CMT) in Mathematics. Additionally, Internalization attitudes were positively predictive of the CMT in Reading while Immersion/Emersion attitudes were negatively predictive. The authors recommend interventions that foster cultural pride and collective unity in young Black men, such that academic success will not be seen as separate from who they need to be in their communities.

High School Students

In a longitudinal quantitative study conducted by Spencer, Noll, Stoltzfus, and Harpalani (2001), 562 African American adolescents from four public middle schools in a metropolitan city in the Southeast were surveyed. The sample consisted of 394 boys and 168 girls from sixth-, seventh-, and eighth-grade classrooms. Academic achievement was measured by the students' national percentile scores on the Iowa Test of Basic Skills. Racial identity was measured using a modified version of the *Racial Identity Attitude Scale* (RIAS) (Parham & Helms, 1985). The RIAS consists of four subscales: *Pre-Encounter, Encounter, Immersion,* and *Internalization.* The authors characterized the subscales as Eurocentric, Transitional, Reactive Afrocentrism, and Proactive Afrocentrism, respectively.

The authors found a negative correlation between Pre-Encounter scores and the Iowa achievement scores, and also a negative correlation between

Immersion scores and the Iowa achievement scores. However, they found evidence for a modest positive correlation between Encounter scores and the Iowa achievement scores, as well as Internalization scores and the Iowa achievement scores. The authors also found that low achievement was more associated with Pre-Encounter (i.e., Eurocentricity) scores, while high achievement was more associated with Internalization (i.e., low Eurocentricity). The authors conclude that their findings support the idea that high-achieving African American students do not identify with acting White values.

College Students

Sellers, Chavous, and Cooke (1998) conducted a quantitative study involving 248 African American college students. The sample included 163 students from a predominantly White public university (PWU) and 85 students from a historically Black private university (HBU). The authors reported that 70.6% of the sample was female, which translates to about 175 females and 73 males. Academic achievement was measured via students' self-reporting their GPA. Racial identity was measured using the *Multidimensional Inventory of Black Identity* (Sellers et al., 1997). The subscales used from the MIBI included the four racial ideology subscales (*Nationalist, Oppressed Minority, Assimilation,* and *Humanist*) and the *Racial Centrality* subscale. There were differences in racial identity by school, with students at the PWU reporting higher Assimilation and Humanist scores but lower Nationalist scores compared to students at the HBU. Assimilation scores were negatively correlated with GPA, while no other dimensions of racial identity were correlated with GPA. An additional statistical analysis indicated that racial centrality was a positive predictor of GPA, while Assimilation scores and Nationalist scores were negatively associated with GPA. Furthermore, individuals for whom race was central had negative associations between Nationalist and Assimilation ideologies with GPA and a positive association between minority ideology and GPA. The authors conclude that racelessness does not appear to be an effective strategy for African American college students. Importantly, they also cite the work of Rowley et al. (1998) to emphasize that racial identity is not a panacea, and that racial identity should play only a relatively minor role in academic achievement in comparison to other factors such as motivation, innate ability, difficulty of grading, and course selection.

Cokley and Moore (2007) conducted a quantitative study that included 274 African American students. The participants included 216 women and 58 men. Academic achievement was measured via students' self-reported GPA. Ethnic identity was measured using the *Multigroup Ethnic Identity Measure* (MEIM) (Phinney, 1992). Racial identity was also measured using the *Racial Centrality* subscale (Sellers et al., 1997).

Focusing on the impact of gender, the authors found ethnic identity and racial centrality were negatively correlated with GPA for men, while ethnic identity was positively correlated with GPA for women. An additional statistical analysis indicated that GPA increased for women with high ethnic identity, but decreased for men with high ethnic identity. The authors conclude that there is a gendered racial and ethnic identity (Oyserman, Bybee, & Terry, 2003) and that African American males are impacted by a cool-pose culture (Majors & Billson, 1992) in which non-academically oriented activities play a more important role in identity and self-esteem than they do for African American females.

Interested in statistically testing a model of academic achievement using the data from the aforementioned study, my graduate student and I conducted another quantitative study with the same data set of 274 students (Cokley & Chapman, 2008). Two subscales were used from the MEIM: ethnic identity and other-group orientation (attitudes toward other ethnic groups). An aspect of racial identity, anti-White attitudes, was also measured using the Immersion-Emersion Anti-White subscale from the CRIS (Vandiver et al., 2002).

We found that other-group orientation was positively correlated with GPA, while anti-White attitudes were negatively correlated with GPA. Ethnic identity was not significantly correlated with GPA. In additional statistical analyses, we found that anti-White attitudes were significantly and negatively predictive of GPA, while ethnic identity was positively and indirectly related to GPA through academic self-concept. We also conducted additional statistical analyses and found that the model predicting academic achievement was statistically weaker when ethnic identity was eliminated. We concluded that even in an indirect role, ethnic identity may be more important for African American academic achievement than anti-White attitudes.

Elion, Wang, Slaney, and French (2012) conducted a quantitative study with a sample of 219 African American college students attending two large public universities from the mid-Atlantic and southern regions. The sample included 105 females and 114 males. Academic achievement was measured via students' self-reported GPA. Racial identity was measured using the *Cross Racial Identity Scale* (CRIS) (Vandiver et al., 2000). The CRIS measures the Expanded Nigrescence theory of William Cross (1991). The CRIS includes the following subscales: *Pre-Encounter Assimilation, Pre-Encounter Miseducation, Pre-Encounter Self-Hatred, Immersion/Emersion Anti-White, Internalization Afrocentric,* and *Internalization Multiculturalist Inclusive.*

While the primary purpose of this study was not to examine the relationship of racial identity and academic achievement, the authors reported results that included this data. The authors found that Pre-Encounter Miseducation was negatively correlated with GPA, while Internalization Multiculturalist Inclusive was positively correlated with GPA. The authors speculate that students in the Miseducation stage could struggle more with feelings of inferiority and inadequacy that may be related to stereotype threat, while concluding that African American individuals with a more mature racial worldview (i.e., Multiculturalist Inclusive) also have higher standards. It is also notable that Immersion-Emersion Anti-White and Internalization Afrocentricity were negatively correlated with GPA (but not statistically significant).

ANALYSIS AND CONCLUSIONS

This brief review of quantitative empirical studies was not intended to be comprehensive or exhaustive. Indeed, I could have reviewed a number of qualitative, ethnographic, and mixed-methods studies that are significant but equally as equivocal in their findings and conclusions (e.g., Bergin & Cooks, 2002; Fordham & Ogbu, 1986; Graham & Anderson, 2008; Nasir, McLaughlin, & Jones, 2009; Wright, 2011). The Fordham and Ogbu article in particular is influential in that it is largely responsible for introducing the "acting White" jargon into academic discourse. This article will be discussed more in depth in the next chapter.

It is difficult to draw definitive conclusions about the relationship between racial and ethnic identity and academic achievement. This brief review underscores the sometimes contradictory findings in the literature. Only a formal meta-analysis (i.e., a quantitative statistical analysis of many studies) would allow for more definitive conclusions to be drawn. Nevertheless, some tentative conclusions may be drawn after careful analysis of this literature. First, it is inappropriate to make any global statements about the relationship between racial and ethnic identity and academic achievement. This is because most conceptualizations of racial and ethnic identity are multidimensional, with each dimension or component having general differences in racial worldviews, ideologies, and attitudes. It is these differences in racial worldviews, ideologies, and attitudes that are most likely to be differentially related to academic achievement.

Related to the previous point, one may tentatively conclude that aspects of racial or ethnic identity that either de-emphasize one's Black identity or internalize miseducated, stereotypical notions of one's Black identity are at risk to be negatively related to academic achievement (Cokley et al., 2011; Nasir et al., 2009). Not taking pride in being Black and/or believing the negative societal messages about being Black (e.g., not intelligent, gangsta, criminal, only good at sports, lazy, etc.) is indicative of a poor self-concept, which psychological research has linked to negative outcomes. Additionally, aspects of Black identity that emphasize an intense love of being Black that is inextricably coupled with White hostility or anti-White attitudes are also likely to be negatively related to academic achievement.

I draw this conclusion knowing that it will not set well with those individuals whose extreme versions of a pro-Black, anti-White mindset have sustained them in their activism and fight for social justice for Black people. Emotions that are associated with these attitudes include pride, rage (at White people and White culture), and guilt (at ever having believed ideas that did not fully liberate Black people) (Cross, 1991). Cross characterized this Black militancy (and related ideological movements such as Black nationalism and Afrocentrism) as being impulsive and emotionally unstable. Furthermore, he characterized the cognitive styles of both Pre-Encounter and Internalization as being in control, logical and rational, while the cognitive style of Immersion-Emersion attitudes (characteristic of Black militants) as being dominated by cognitive dissonance and emotionality. Perhaps the emotional lability that characterizes pro-Black, anti-White attitudes interferes with the individual's ability to focus on academics. Psychological research has shown that negative emotions such as anger and anxiety are often negatively linked with academic achievement (Gumora & Arsenio, 2002; Valiente, Swanson, & Eisenberg, 2012). Another reason that attitudes related to Black militancy may be negatively related to academic achievement could be linked to personality traits. There is evidence that certain personality traits such as conscientiousness and openness to experience are positively predictive of academic outcomes (Noftle & Robins, 2007). Attitudes that characterize certain forms of Black militancy, particularly as related to attitudes toward White people and White culture, can probably be safely described as not being open to experiences with White people.

Finally, aspects of Black identity that embrace being Black and being connected to family and community and also being aware of racism, while also valuing and embracing multiculturalism and the experiences other racial and ethnic groups, are also more likely to be positively related to academic achievement. This is probably related to the previous observation that the personality trait openness to experience has been positively linked to academic outcomes. Additionally, rather than expend emotional energy on hating White people, this construction of Black identity is more "school-oriented and socially conscious" (Nasir et al., 2009, p. 92) and promotes academic identification and higher academic achievement (Cokley et al., 2011).

The third tentative conclusion to be drawn is that there are probably developmental differences that impact the relationship. Specifically, it appears that a positive relationship is more likely to occur among younger students (i.e., pre–high school). In other words, the academic achievement of younger students is more likely to increase as aspects of their Black identity increases. One possible reason is that younger students are less susceptible to conformity and peer pressure than early adolescents (Brown, Lohr, & McClenahan, 1986; Clasen & Brown, 1985). The pressures surrounding being popular and cool, while present with middle school students, is not as intense as with high school students. Younger students are also generally more identified with academics than adolescents (Osborne, 1999). Thus, it is possible that younger pre-adolescent African American students have had less exposure to the negative messages related to Black identity and academic achievement, and thus are more open to integrating academic achievement into their racial identity. High school students appear to be the most vulnerable for having aspects of their Black identity be negatively linked to academic achievement. It would appear that special efforts need to be in place, in the form of changes in the type of curriculum taught and pedagogy, or having targeted cultural after-school enrichment programs, to counter the potentially negative effects of peer pressure. When students make the decision to go to college, they have already identified with school to a certain degree and can be assumed to have more positive attitudes toward academics. The exposure to Black-oriented student organizations and Black Studies or multicultural classes will increase the likelihood that students' racial and ethnic identity will be positively linked to their academic achievement. It is probably safe to say that those Black student organizations and classes that focus on Black pride and achievements rather than anti-White sentiments, as well as foster an appreciation for multiculturalism, will be more successful academically.

Finally, I would be remiss if I did not point out some of the major limitations of this body of work. Virtually all of the studies are correlational in nature rather than experimental. Essentially, we are looking at associations between these variables. In other words, as racial or ethnic identity increases, academic achievement tends to either increase or decrease. However, there is a major methodological limitation that should be noted. Based on the research design of the studies, we cannot conclude that racial or ethnic identity *causes* academic achievement. Furthermore, the strength of the relationship between racial and ethnic identity and academic achievement (referred to by statisticians as *effect size*) in the reviewed studies is between small and medium. This underscores the point made by Rowley et al. (1998) when they stated that racial identity is not a panacea. Sellers et al. (1998) go on to state that even for students for whom race is a very important part of their identity, racial identity should play only a minor role in their academic achievement. In the final analysis, I agree with their statement, as the data appear to support that position. Instead of overinterpreting data to be consistent with whatever our ideological proclivities are, we should draw all conclusions strictly on what can be reasonably inferred from the best available research and data. Regarding the question "What is the relationship of racial and ethnic identity to academic achievement?" the best answer is simply "It depends on what aspect of racial and ethnic is being examined, what year in school is the student, what gender is the student, etc." There is no one all-encompassing, definitive answer, so any attempt to present it as such is naïve and disingenuous.

In the next chapter I explore some of the most provocative and controversial narratives about African American students related to the themes of acting White, victimhood, and Black anti-intellectualism. I demonstrate that many of the conclusions drawn about the psychology of African American students are strikingly not psychological at all. Rather, they are part of a larger web of criticisms that serves to perpetuate deficit notions of Black students and ultimately Black culture.

3

Acting White and Oppositional Culture: Missing the Forest for the Trees

On July 7, 2004, an Illinois state senator and candidate for the U.S. Senate named Barack Obama delivered the keynote address for the Democratic National Convention in Boston, Massachusetts. He was a relatively unknown politician on the national scene, but was viewed as a rising star within the Democratic Party. He was a highly educated, Harvard-trained lawyer and former University of Chicago professor. He was also an incredible speaker. The fact that he was African American, while not explicitly focused on by the Democratic Party, was certainly noted by news organizations and media outlets. In an applause-filled, rousing speech that introduced him to the U.S. public and made him an instant political celebrity, Senator Obama made what many consider to be one of his most brilliant speeches. Among the many topics that he addressed included education. He made the following comments:

> Go into any inner-city neighborhood, and folks will tell you that government alone can't teach kids to learn. . . . They know that parents have to teach, that children can't achieve unless we raise their expectations and turn off the television sets and eradicate the slander that says a black youth with a book is acting white.

In seconds, Senator Obama gave credence to, and perpetuated, the widely reported yet hotly debated notion that Black students do not try to excel in school because of the fear of being labeled as "acting white." No other characterization has received more media attention, been more damning for any group of students, and contributed more to the belief that Black students are anti-intellectual, than the so-called "acting White" phenomenon. If you type "acting white" in Google, approximately 312 million results are generated. Even the most casual observer has heard the phrase and knows that it typically refers to an attitude that is believed to be pervasive among African American students.

The discourse surrounding the so-called acting White phenomenon is part of a larger deficit narrative that is used to characterize not only African American students, but Black culture more generally. What makes these commentaries especially significant is that they are often made by certain Black academics and other high-profile Black individuals (e.g., Bill Cosby, John McWhorter, John Ogbu, Shelby Steele, and Juan Williams). It would be easy to characterize these individuals as political conservatives; however, this is a much too simplistic and inaccurate categorization. While the journalist Juan Williams and academic Shelby Steele are self-proclaimed Black conservatives, Bill Cosby is a confirmed Democrat, and John McWhorter, who appears to be socially conservative, describes himself as a cranky liberal Democrat. The political affiliation of the anthropology scholar John Ogbu, to the best of my knowledge, was unknown or at least never made public. Political ideology does not fully explain why these criticisms of Black culture are made.

In this chapter I critically interrogate the idea of acting White along with other reductionist characterizations (i.e., oppositional culture) that have been repeatedly used to describe and characterize African American students. Specifically, I critique the work of the prominent anthropology scholars John Ogbu and Signithia Fordham, whose research has been the most responsible for the narrative surrounding Black students and acting White. I also briefly review qualitative and quantitative social science evidence that both complicates and challenges the idea that the fear of acting White is what is most responsible for Black student underachievement.

DECONSTRUCTING THE ACTING WHITE THESIS: AN AFRICENTRIC CRITIQUE*

Perhaps no other scholar has been as influential and controversial on matters of African American educational underachievement as the late educational anthropologist John Ogbu. After all, it was Ogbu, along with his colleague and former student Signithia Fordham, who initially canonized the idea that the pursuit of high academic achievement is shunned by African American students because it is associated with behaviors deemed to be acting White. Fordham and Ogbu (1986) describe a theory whereby involuntary minorities like African Americans develop an oppositional collective and cultural identity, where authentic Blackness is perceived to be rejecting anything (including academic pursuits) that approximates White American values and behaviors. No other idea about Black student achievement has been as codified in the collective public consciousness as the idea of Black students not doing well in school because of the fear of acting White.

What makes Ogbu's work so compelling that it has been the subject of countless papers, articles, and academic debates? I believe that, in part, its popularity stems from its reliance on an epistemologically Eurocentric analysis. Scholars, educators, and laypeople are often easily seduced by overly simplistic

---

*Portions of this section were previously published in the online journal *Texas Education Review*. Cokley, K. (2013). Deconstructing Ogbu's acting White thesis: An Africentric critique. *Texas Education Review*, 1, 154–163.

catchphrases or explanations to understand complex behavioral, psychological, and cultural phenomena. While the principle of parsimony (Occam's razor) requires that minimum assumptions and the simplest explanation be chosen to explain a given phenomenon, it does not mean that surface-level observations are easily reduced to surface-level explanations. In other words, observing and/or recording African American students labeling a high-achieving African American student as acting White does not warrant a characterization of African American academic underperformance as a response to the fear of acting White. Relatedly, recording interviews of African American students who fail to rank studying hard as a high priority does not automatically warrant a fear of acting White label. While I have had several African American students admit that at some point they were teased as children or teenagers for acting White, this phenomenon was invariably much more complicated and nuanced than simply an indictment of their academic performance. In fact, as I will argue, this acting White phenomenon often has very little to do with attitudes toward academic performance proper.

In spite of his earnest attempt to challenge blaming the victim and culture of poverty deficit theorists, some would argue that nonetheless, Ogbu's analysis is rooted in a blaming the victim and deficit model of African American culture. To be fair to Ogbu, his work has not always been fairly critiqued. Foley (2004) points out that Ogbu's work has often been used and abused by conservative and liberal ideologues to promote their own sociopolitical agendas. For example, Foley argues that it is not accurate to characterize Ogbu as a deficit thinker because Ogbu believes that the dysfunctional aspects of African American culture are adaptations to the destructive legacy of racial oppression, and not inherent cultural traits. Foley's attempt to rehabilitate and rescue this underlying premise of Ogbu's work should be noted and is admirable. However, in this instance I think Foley is being overly generous toward Ogbu, and is being surprisingly naïve as an educational anthropologist himself. Let us not be misguided. Deficit theories assume that the people in question have problems to be solved, and they draw correlations between the levels of educational achievement and the amount of motivation of the people and their culture (Claveria & Alonso, 2003). In short, deficit theories do not discriminate between notions of dysfunctional adaptations to racial oppression or inherent cultural traits. Whether mutable or immutable, the fundamental belief is still that there is a deficiency in African American culture. Lundy (2003) argues that the belief that Black culture needs to be altered is essentially a culture-of-poverty argument. Simply put, a rose called by any other name is still a rose. Additionally, as we have seen, Black public intellectuals like John McWhorter have cited Ogbu when making broad sweeping indictments of African American culture as having an ethos of anti-intellectualism (McWhorter, 2000). Lundy characterizes Ogbu as using a "sleight of hand" by being careful not to blame Black children for having deficient cognitive abilities. Instead, Ogbu simply makes a cultural analysis by stating that Black children have deficient values and motivations which prevent them from excelling academically.

While it may be believed that Ogbu minimizes or downplays the role of racial discrimination in African American student outcomes, Foster (2004) states that Ogbu acknowledges the roles of both community and system forces in understanding the African American responses to schooling. Ogbu, according to Foster, takes the existence of racial discrimination as a given, but consciously chooses to focus his attention on the role of African Americans "in their own academic failure" (p. 372). Ogbu purports to be interested in African American agency in the context of systematic discrimination, but this claim is misleading at best, and disingenuous at worst. Ogbu does not appear to understand what African American agency really means, and makes no coherent theoretical argument about African American student agency.

Interestingly, and perhaps understandably, over the years Ogbu became more defensive about his work. While the best of scientific discourse requires the ebb and flow of constant intellectual interrogations, with theorists responding to the weight of rival plausible hypotheses in light of mounting evidence and alternative interpretations, Ogbu remained relatively impervious to other legitimate interpretations of the phenomenon he labeled acting White. In his last published manuscript, Ogbu (2004) claims that his critics have misinterpreted the problem by constructing a different problem than the one he and Fordham originally discussed in their 1986 article. Ironically, Ogbu claims that his critics "ignore the historical and community contexts of Black students' behavior and focus almost exclusively on the transactions between the students and their school" (p. 2). One could make a similar statement about Ogbu, and argue that he underestimates the importance of the racialized transactions and interactions between students and their predominantly White teachers while focusing much more on oppositional culture, parental shortcomings and the negative influence of peer culture.

For the sake of civil academic discourse, I will not belabor Ogbu's defensiveness of his work. Suffice it to say that while he may have had legitimate concerns about the mischaracterization and misinterpretation of his work, it is also clear that, as two reviewers noted, his final contribution reads more like a "defense of an entrenched position than objective social science research" (Charles & Torres, 2004).

In defending his work from charges of blaming the victim, Ogbu stated that his work is not politically correct (Burdman, 2003). By that, presumably, he meant that any analysis that locates the cause of African American students' underachievement in (1) the attitudes and behaviors of the students themselves, and (2) the lack of appropriate guidance and support from their parents, will automatically be viewed as blaming the victim. Ogbu argued that by virtue of his anthropological training, he does not think that any culture or language is superior to any other culture or language. Therefore, the language that is spoken in the homes of many Black students, Ebonics, was not viewed by Ogbu as inferior. However, Ogbu, like many African Americans, believed that to be successful and accomplish certain goals in this country means that one has to adopt the norms of White culture. Ogbu believed that Blacks could instrumentally adopt the norms of White culture without losing their Black identity. To the extent that Black students do not adopt the norms of White culture, Ogbu believed that Black students are contributors to and participants in their academic shortcomings.

In making this argument, in some ways Ogbu sounds like several prominent Black academics and cultural critics. John McWhorter, who I will discuss at length later, made some similar comments in his book *Losing the Race: Self-Sabotage in Black America*, where he argues that Black students that he has taught have not had the right attitudes and have not engaged in the appropriate behaviors to be academically successful. Shelby Steele (1991) made similar comments in his book *The Content of Our Character*, where he argued that an emphasis on racial victimization has created a social psychology among Blacks that de-emphasizes individual responsibility and emphasizes entitlements based on internalized beliefs of Black inferiority. Even Bill Cosby (who, as previously mentioned, cannot be characterized as politically conservative), has joined the growing chorus of critical Black voices by commenting on what he believes to be the poor language skills of Black youth and their failure to take their education seriously. While the comments of McWhorter, Steele, and Cosby were not without controversy, they were privileged by the cultural and social location of each individual. In short, they have "insider status" by virtue of their African American identity. Using Ogbu's terms, they belong to a caste-like, involuntary minority.

Although Ogbu was Black and African, his experience as a voluntary immigrant minority did not provide him the intellectual authority or capital to fully comprehend the inner dynamics of African American culture. Although he apparently felt that not being African American afforded him a level of objectivity that may escape African American scholars and commentators, it was this phenomenological disconnection from his work that placed him squarely in the logic and reasoning of Eurocentric scholarship. Ogbu used ideas of collective identity, acting White, and the history of Black oppression to understand and explain Black student underachievement without interrogating the possibility that his observation of the rejection of so-called White attitudes and behaviors may have been part of a larger movement of African American agency that is demanding of more culturally appropriate and relevant education.

Mwalimu Shujaa has observed that the community of African-descended people in the United States makes a distinction between education and schooling (Shujaa, 2003). Shujaa notes that while it is often assumed that getting an education is the by-product of going to school, people of African descent understand that schooling "can both serve as well as betray their interests" (Shujaa, 2003, p. 245). Shujaa defines schooling as "a process intended to perpetuate and maintain the society's existing power relations and the institutional structures that support those arrangements" while defining education as a "means of providing for the intergenerational transmission of values, beliefs, traditions, customs, rituals and sensibilities along with the knowledge of why these things must be sustained." Shujaa goes on to say that "Through education we learn how to determine what is in our interests, distinguish our interests from those of others, and recognize when our interests are consistent and inconsistent with those of others" (p. 246).

While Ogbu's work can be, and has been, critiqued on the basis of methodological and interpretive problems as well as a selective and perhaps self-serving reading of history, I offer additional critical observations and interpretations of his work that are informed by my knowledge, training, and orientation as an African-centered psychologist. First, Ogbu appeared to lack a thorough understanding of how subtle racialized student-teacher interactions significantly contribute to the collective psychology of African American students. Second, I believe that there is another interpretation for the so-called acting White phenomenon, one that involves a critical analysis regarding the purpose of education. A critical discussion of what the purpose of education should be for African Americans provides the proper context with which to begin to understand the nature of the attitudes and behaviors of African American students as responses to a personally and culturally irrelevant education.

My biggest problem with Ogbu was his myopic construction of the problem. To the extent that his observations of the acting White phenomenon are accurate, I believe that he failed to adequately understand that the concerns of the Black community are real. In the 1998 PBS documentary *The Two Nations of Black America*, prominent African American scholar Henry Louis Gates states that he shares more in common with his fellow White Harvard colleagues than with the average Black person on the streets. Africentric and other progressive African American scholars and academics see these types of sentiments as polarizing and distancing middle- and upper-class Blacks from working-class Blacks. These sentiments might also be seen as examples of the tensions between schooling and education. If the process of schooling results in Blacks becoming more socially and culturally distant from the Black community, it is no wonder that there would be mixed or negative attitudes about school. This is why Shujaa makes the distinction between schooling and education.

In my Politics of Black Identity class, I show the Two Nations of Black America documentary. Narrated by Henry Louis "Skip" Gates, the documentary explores the chasm between the upper and lower classes of Black America and offers commentary about why the chasm exists. Toward the end of the documentary, Gates makes the comment about sharing more in common with his fellow White colleagues than the average Black person on the street. At one point during the documentary, a Black male gangbanger is being interviewed. Gates comments that this man seemed like a Martian to him. Such was the degree to which Gates could not relate to him. During the class discussion following the video, the majority of students thought that Gates came across as bourgeois and condescending. In an interesting discussion with my teaching assistant (a Nigerian American woman) after class, she astutely hypothesized that part of the reason that people had such negative reactions to Gates was because essentially he was articulating sentiments that many educated, middle-class Blacks privately share about their social and cultural distance from lower- and working-class Blacks.

The issue among African Americans is not primarily a lack of encouragement for academic achievement, although this certainly may exist amongst some African Americans. The issue is also not primarily the possession of negative cultural attitudes that deflates Black achievement, although again, this may be observed on a surface level among some African Americans. Instead, I believe that there is, and always has been, a fundamental concern among African Americans that the pursuit of education vis-à-vis schooling not result in an existential disconnection from our families, from our communities, and from our culture. The many interviews conducted by Ogbu and his associates revealed attitudes and behaviors among African American students that were contraindicative for making good grades. These attitudes and behaviors were labeled as a fear of acting White. This was an easy and, frankly, rather surface-level interpretation of his data. Another interpretation, one that requires a deeper and more informed connection to African American culture, argues that there are social and psychological mechanisms in place in the culture that seek to maintain the collective ties that bind. In other words, when individuals start to stray from their cultural moorings, forces within the culture will seek to, for lack of a better phrase, attempt to bring them back home. The acting White phenomenon may be a subtle way of ensuring that African Americans do not become caught up in White socialization that results from schooling. An understudied perspective that needs to be explored is that African American students are not interested in participating in and perpetuating systems of the White status quo that result in a compromised sense of cultural connection and Black identity.

ACTING WHITE: BEYOND SCHOOL ACHIEVEMENT

While the fear of acting White has become the de facto explanation given to explain Black student underachievement, several studies have been conducted that present a more complicated picture. In one study, Bergin and Cooks (2002) cited several studies (e.g., Ainsworth-Darnell & Downey, 1998; Cook & Ludwig, 1998) that contradicted several aspects of the acting White thesis (e.g., levels of school effort, value of education, academic alienation). Bergin and Cooks noted that the studies on which the acting White thesis became popularized (i.e., Fordham, 1988, 1996; Fordham & Ogbu, 1986) were based on data from one predominantly Black high school in Washington, D.C. They wanted to expand on the study, so they collected data from several types of schools including private and public, predominantly White, predominantly Black, and racially mixed. They conducted a qualitative study with a sample of 38 high school students. Out of the 38 students, 28 were in a scholarship incentive program that required having a B average, and 10 were in a comparison program. The students included African Americans, Mexican Americans, and mixed-race individuals. The research questions included the following: "Did students report avoiding academic achievement in order to avoid appearing to act white?" and "Did they perceive that they had given up ethnic identity in order to do well in school?"

Bergin and Cooks reported that the students had several descriptions of acting White, which fell along the themes of speech, music, dress, school, and other behaviors. Examples of speech included talking proper, not using slang and not cursing, and using big words. Examples of dress included not wearing tennis shoes, dressing like a preppie, wearing a tie, and buttoning your shirt instead of letting your chest hang out. Examples of school included sucking up to the teachers, working up to your potential, getting good grades, and always doing your work. Examples of other behaviors included dating White girls, having lots of White friends, and acting stuck up.

Based on the responses of the students, Bergin and Cooks concluded that they did not avoid academic achievement to avoid accusations of acting White. This was evident by the students having an overall grade point average of 3.3. Additionally, the authors concluded that the students did not perceive themselves as giving up their ethnic identity. One particularly important finding was that students in predominantly White settings were less likely to be accused of acting White, while students in predominantly Black settings were more likely to be accused of acting White when their behaviors went beyond high achievement. Another important observation was that while doing well in school was often seen as an indicator of acting White, it was almost never a sufficient indicator. The students spent more time discussing other behavioral indicators of acting White than they did on simply getting good grades.

CULTURAL-ECOLOGICAL THEORY AND OPPOSITIONAL CULTURE

Ogbu's most influential scholarly contribution was introducing his cultural-ecological theory. The motivation behind the development of cultural-ecological theory was Ogbu's concern that cross-cultural research was using models based on the experiences of the White middle class as the basis of comparison of minority groups such as urban Blacks (Ogbu, 1981). Using a universal model based on White middle-class behaviors resulted in, among other things, minority parents' teaching skills being viewed as deficient (Ogbu, 1981). At the core of cultural-ecological theory is the premise that human competencies are situated within culturally defined adult tasks. In other words, all cultures have successfully performed tasks (e.g., child-rearing techniques) in ways that produced competent adults to meet specific environmental demands. While this observation has been readily made when comparing across cultures, according to Ogbu, it had not been sufficiently acknowledged that it applies to populations within the United States. Furthermore, cultural-ecological theory requires that cultures be studied on their own terms, with no evaluations of good or bad, or deficient or not deficient, being made (Ogbu, 1981).

Applying cultural-ecological theory to Black American culture (what Ogbu refers to as the "ghetto case"), Ogbu reviewed ethnographic studies and other literature to identify six reoccurring identity themes. The themes included: (1) oppositional collective identity, (2) oppositional cultural frame of reference, and (3) strategies for coping with the burden of acting White (Ogbu & Simons, 1988). Ogbu cited several examples as evidence of oppositional culture identity throughout the history of Black Americans, including (1) the frequency with which Black authors cite Du Bois's double consciousness, (2) shifts in identity labels (Negro to Colored to Black), (3) the use of linguistic labels such as "soul," "brother," or "sister" while using negative labels to describe White men, (4) the use of other cultural and dialect frames of reference to highlight differences between Blacks and Whites (e.g., styles of walking, gesturing, and the use of Black vernacular English), and (5) the expression of disdain at emulating the White man. Ogbu along with Signithia Fordham theorized that oppositional cultural identity contributed to the lower academic achievement of Black students through the fear of being perceived as "acting White" (Fordham & Ogbu, 1986).

The oppositional culture thesis, along with the notion of acting White, has become the de facto reasons used by teachers, scholars, politicians, and educational pundits to explain the causes of Black underachievement. As the beginning of the chapter illustrates, even the president of the United States perpetuates the narrative that goes along with an uncritical acceptance of these explanations. However, mounting social science research challenges the empirical support of these explanations.

DEVALUING SCHOOL OR LACK OF SKILLS?

In a comprehensive quantitative empirical study examining the oppositional culture thesis, Harris (2011) found that Black students actually value school more than White students although they do not perform as well academically. Using a series of statistical analyses, Harris did not find support for the oppositional culture hypothesis. He argues that the reason Black kids underperform academically is not because they do not value school, but rather because they do not have the skills to be successful (Harris & Robinson, 2007). By emphasizing skills, he is not arguing that Black students do not possess the innate intelligence to be academically successful; instead, he is arguing that they have not mastered some of the basic skills in their early education that they would need in order to be successful in the classroom. His overall message is simple yet powerful: Black kids do not want to fail in school. What is particularly compelling about Harris's work and analysis is that he is not a scholar who could easily be classified as an activist, or a scholar with an obvious ideological agenda. He is a scholar who draws conclusions based on sound empirical data. And based on his careful empirical study of what is supposed to be a phenomenon of oppositional culture, he finds that the data do not support the presumed widespread prevalence of an oppositional culture.

TYPES OF OPPOSITIONALITY TO HIGH ACHIEVEMENT

In one of the most rigorous and thoughtful qualitative examinations of the acting White thesis, Tyson, Darity, and Castellino (2005) interviewed 40 Black students and 36 White students across eight middle and high schools. Students were chosen who were in rigorous courses and programs. In all but one of the schools, Black students were underrepresented in these courses and programs. Contrary to the assumptions of oppositional culture, the authors found that Black students expressed a desire to do well in school. They wanted to do well when they were in advanced classes, and they also wanted to do well in regular classes. In fact, in instances when Black students avoided the advanced classes, it was because they were concerned about their grades being lowered. The authors argued that this went against oppositional culture, because the students were so concerned about their grades that they took less challenging classes. If oppositional culture were really in effect, the students would not be taking regular classes to get As because they would not care about getting As at all. Tyson et al. (2005) found that none of the Black students interviewed at the schools exhibited an ambivalence about achievements. They also did not find widespread pressure to underachieve among Black students because of a fear of acting White. In fact, only one of the eight schools had evidence of a burden of acting White.

While Tyson et al. found very little data to support the acting White and oppositional culture hypotheses, they are careful to not categorically dismiss the existence of these attitudes. Regarding oppositional culture, they identify three distinct types of oppositionality to high achievement. First, there is a *general oppositional culture* where high-achieving students are referred to as nerds, dorks, brainiacs, and other similar terms. Second, there is a *racialized oppositional culture* that occurs among some Black students where high-achieving students are referred to as acting White. Third, there is a *class-based oppositional culture* where high achieving students are referred to as snooty, snobby, preppy, high and mighty, and other similar terms. The authors found that in the one school where a racialized oppositional culture existed, there were stark differences in socioeconomic status between Black and White students. The advanced courses in this school were comprised of White students who were socioeconomically privileged, and a few Black students who typically were not. So when underachieving Black students in this school referred to high-achieving Black students as acting White, it was within a context where a sizable gap existed in the socioeconomic status of Black and White students. Tyson et al. suggest that the racial disparity in students who take advanced classes affects how Black students perceive those classes and who takes them. They know that students in the advanced classes are seen as the students who are expected to be successful, and who are provided more support to be successful. This in turn breeds resentment among lower-achieving students, which among Black students can result in a racialized oppositional culture where they take out their frustrations on their high-achieving peers.

In their discussion, Tyson et al. (2005) state that the perception of high-achieving students among both Black and White students is sometimes less than positive. Both high-achieving Black and White students become the target of resentment when they take on what is interpreted as an air of arrogance or superiority. For White students, this perceived air of arrogance is based on class, while for Black students, it becomes racialized. Both Black and White students experienced a general oppositional culture where they were referred to by names such as dork or nerd. This experience is a normal part of adolescent development for most teenagers. The authors argue that Fordham and Ogbu (1986) were so focused on what made Black students different in their achievement that they ignored important similarities between Blacks and Whites regarding the burden of high achievement.

The authors conclude that inconsistencies in research findings about oppositional culture could be resolved if researchers recognize that context matters. Instead of focusing on the culture of schools, more focus should be placed on the role of school structures (e.g., tracking students by ability, gap in Black and White median income) in creating and perpetuating animosity among high and low achieving students. They suggest that future studies in this area would be best served by providing more details on students' experiences that distinguish acting White from other instances of general or class-based oppositional culture that occur among most adolescents.

ACTING WHITE REVISITED: MISCHARACTERIZATION, MISINTERPRETATION, OR MISSING THE BOAT?

Perhaps no other phrase is more associated with the idea that Black students do not value school and are anti-intellectual than "acting White." It is important

that an accurate context is provided for how the acting White thesis was introduced into the scientific literature and public's consciousness. After Ogbu's
death in 2003, a tremendous amount of scholarly focus was once again placed
on his work and legacy. Forgotten in all of the attention placed on Ogbu was
the role of his collaborator, Signithia Fordham. In her 2008 article published in
Anthropology and Education Quarterly, Fordham reminds us how the acting White
thesis was introduced into the scientific literature. In this article, she reflected on
her original 1986 study and the tremendous impact it had on scholarly studies
and media reports about African American student achievement, and ultimately
on her career. According to Google Scholar, the study has been cited over
3,090 times, which by academic standards is quite amazing (especially for a social
scientist).

In an edgy and at times biting article, Fordham lamented about what she
believes is the misrepresentation and mischaracterization of her work. She stated
that in her original 1986 study, her description of the phenomenon among Black
students was the *burden of acting White*; however, scholars and media pundits
have repeatedly referred to her description as the *fear of acting White*. Fordham
says that burden connotes carrying a heavy load, which was the stress that she
was trying to convey occurs among academically successful Black students, while
fear connotes a sense of anxiety. Fordham believes that changing the word burden to fear essentially changes the actual phenomenon she observed and
described. This is one of the main ways Fordham believes that academics and
pundits have appropriated, distorted, and refuted her theoretical claims. She
expresses an annoyance that critics have largely avoided the central points
of her theoretical claims about race being a forced performance on African
American students. By this she presumably means that in order to be validated,
African American students are expected to perform and behave in the ways that
are representative of the dominant White culture. This would include an
embracing of school and valuing of education. However, Fordham notes that
the reality of structural limitations (a euphemism for racism and discrimination)
actually contribute to oppositional culture and thus make oppositional culture a
rational response for African American students. Again, Fordham is clearly
annoyed that scholars and media pundits have misread her.

Before going over more examples that Fordham uses to support her belief in
her work being mischaracterized, I should point out that she is especially critical
of (I would say angered by) what she refers to as sexist practices of male researchers who credited Ogbu rather than her. According to Fordham, the ethnographic
study on which the 1986 article was about was based on her dissertation. Fordham says that Ogbu only lent his name to the project to help her get published;
however, she says that the sexist practices of male scholars minimize her role in
the research, and in fact, scholars often say the citation Ogbu and Fordham when
it should be Fordham and Ogbu. Feeling guilty when I first read this, I looked

back at one of my articles focusing on Ogbu. Being a stickler on citations (I am editor-in-chief of a journal), I was relieved to see that I rightly cited Fordham and Ogbu. In point of fact, all of the sources that I saw using the search terms "Ogbu and Fordham 1986" actually included the correct citation of Fordham and Ogbu. However, I cannot deny the spirit of her main point: my article was written as though Ogbu were the primary contributor with Fordham being the collaborator who was brought on. When most people talk about the acting White thesis, Ogbu is generally the focus rather than Fordham. I honestly never gave much thought to this point, but Fordham is absolutely right. Sexism, whether conscious or unconscious, is alive and well. This sexism is important to acknowledge because it provides a context for understanding what becomes increasingly apparent—her feelings of resentment about playing second fiddle to a male scholar who was given the credit for her work that he, at least in part, appeared to disagree with (Fordham, 2004).

Another example of how Fordham believes her work has been misread and mischaracterized is how (according to her) scholars and media pundits mischaracterize her work as focusing on the academic struggles of African American students, when her study actually focused on academically successful African American students. I initially set out to try to substantiate her claims, but realized that it would be a much larger and more arduous task than I had envisioned. I have chosen to accept this as her truth and that this is what she genuinely believes without the benefit on having done a content analysis of every time her name and acting White are mentioned together. She apparently has some form of data to support her stance, and I frankly do not have the time or inclination to fact-check her on this point, especially given that there is likely to be some disagreement on what constitutes mischaracterization. However, I will point out that her claim could be challenged as one of the perceptual differences in interpretation of media reports. For example, a Google search including the terms "Signithia Fordham and acting White" led me to a 1990 archived article in the New York Times. The very first sentence of the article references Black students performing poorly because of a sense that academic success is a sellout to the White world. The article was clearly focused on Black students' underachievement. However, Fordham is quoted as saying the following: "Fear of acting White and fear of becoming the other was a motivating factor in underachievement in the school context." Assuming this quote accurately reflects what was said by Fordham, we can see two problems. First, it would appear that Fordham herself was guilty for changing (and sometimes using interchangeably) the phrases "burden of acting White" and "fear of acting White." Second, it would not be a mischaracterization of her work if scholars and pundits situated her analysis within the context of Black students' underachievement. Fordham does that herself, and one can accurately characterize her work within the context of Black students' underachievement without specifically mentioning that she focused on academically successful students. If Fordham is going to call out scholars and media pundits for this supposed mischaracterization, she should also call out herself. Of course, I do not really think she should call out herself, or anyone else for that matter, on this particular issue. She seems to be grasping at straws here.

Fordham argues that the central point made in her 1986 article with Ogbu was that the burden of being accused of acting White was a major reason why Black students do poorly in school. She defines acting White as "an epithet to convey the response of African Americans to the institutionalization of norms and other cultural practices that are generated and imposed by the dominant society" (Fordham & Ogbu, 1986, p. 242). While Fordham appears to be critical of all scholars and media pundits who she believes have mischaracterized this central point of her work, she seems to hold a special contempt for quantitative researchers who try to examine the acting White thesis using quantitative methods. She makes several pointed criticisms about quantitative research, some of which are just extensions of the old philosophical debate between the merits of quantitative versus qualitative methods. For example, Fordham is critical of quantitative researchers (especially economists and psychologists) who only use surveys to ask students about their personal opinions. Instead Fordham, like a true ethnographer and many qualitative researchers, believes that it would be better to observe students in their homes, at school, and doing community activities. To demonstrate the rigor of her research methods, Fordham shares methodological details about her study. She conducted a two-year ethnographic study and a one-year quantitative study in which a 55-page questionnaire was administered to more than 700 students. Thus she conducted a mixed-methods study, which would presumably yield interesting quantitative and qualitative results. However, Fordham does not appear to have ever published the quantitative data in any peer-reviewed journal. I was unable to locate any quantitative studies in the Eric and Psych Info Databases, both of which include her other articles. This fact alone makes her criticism of quantitative researchers look somewhat specious and more ideologically driven than I am sure she would acknowledge.

Continuing with her criticisms of quantitative researchers, Fordham says that their approach does not capture the fundamental issue of the relationship between academic performance and conformity to Black identity. She does not believe that academic performance (or, for that matter, Black identity) can be captured using the methods of self-report that are so often employed by quantitative psychologists and economists. The use of self-reports, Fordham argues, to prove or disprove the acting White thesis is "indefensible" and produces "bad science." Once again, true to her anthropological training as an ethnographer, Fordham believes that only looking at students' interactions with each other (via self-report or observation) is limited. She believes that researchers should look at the interactions between students and teachers, as well as the mismatch between the culture of the home and community and that of the school. Aside from her methodological rigidity and intolerance of quantitative methods, she raises some interesting and important points for consideration. The cultural mismatch between the home and community and that of the school is a perspective that is being examined by psychologists. In a quantitative study, Tyler, Boykin, Miller, and Hurley (2006) found that African American students and their parents had significantly stronger preferences for classroom activities that emphasized communalism and verve (i.e., the propensity for energetic body language and expression [Boykin, 1983]) rather than individualism and competition. This research is consistent with other studies that identify the need for teachers to engage in culturally responsive or relevant teaching (Gay, 2000; Ladson-Billings, 1995), presumably to reduce the incompatibility of mainstream school culture with the home and community cultures of African American students. Furthermore, research by Howard University professor Wade Boykin has shown a consistent pattern of Black children improving in academic performance, motivation, and engagement when aspects of African American culture are incorporated into learning tasks (Allen & Boykin, 1992; Bailey & Boykin, 2001; Boykin & Allen, 1988; Boykin & Cunningham, 2001).

Fordham continues her withering critique of quantitative methods when she argues that quantitative scholars fail to problematize the categories embedded in their data. According to Fordham, this makes it impossible for quantitative scholars to address cultural issues such as the role of Black identity. Psychologists have, in fact, problematized the categories of race and ethnicity in data (e.g., Betancourt & Lopez, 1993; Phinney, 1996; Zuckerman, 1990). Here Fordham is apparently unaware of the vast literature in quantitative psychology that addresses the conceptual and methodological problems associated with the categories of race and ethnicity. Furthermore, as reviewed in Chapter 2, there is a body of literature examining the role of Black identity in Black student achievement. Fordham is critical of economists and psychologists because she believes they simply count outcomes and then try to explain patterns through variables in their data sets. She contrasts this approach to that of her discipline, anthropology, where she says that both anthropologists and sociologists seek to "probe the complex, dialectical process through which racial inequality is reproduced in school" (p. 242).

It is not unusual for scholars to have methodological preferences that reflect the nature of their disciplinary training. I do not fault Fordham for her ethnographic sensibilities because, after all, she is an anthropologist. However, I do believe that her criticisms of quantitative researchers are unnecessarily excessive. One or two pointed critiques about the limitations of quantitative methods to examine the acting White thesis would have been enough to make her point, but Fordham seems intent on categorically dismissing all quantitative efforts to study this phenomenon. Taking another shot at quantitative researchers, Fordham expresses concern that survey approaches to examining acting White confine the phenomenon to simply valuing or devaluing academic achievement. As any quantitative researcher knows, constructs or phenomena have to be operationalized in order to be studied quantitatively. There are always measurement limitations in the operationalization of any construct. Put another way, there is never a perfect way of measuring a construct such as self-esteem. For every researcher who believes the Rosenberg Self-Esteem Scale is a good measure of self-esteem, there will be another researcher who thinks the same scale is flawed and limited.

Perhaps I am reacting so strongly to Fordham's criticism because she is essentially talking about me and the way that I have conducted research. Several researchers, myself included, have used attitudes pertaining to the valuing or devaluing of academic achievement as being consistent with the fear or burden of acting White. Fordham is basically saying that confining the examination of acting White to valuing or devaluing academic achievement misses entirely her point about race as performance, and specifically how African American students are expected to perform Whiteness. She continues by saying that the methodological practice of assuming that valuing academic success is the only criterion of acting White is not really a study of acting White.

I strongly disagree with Fordham's basic premise. As quantitative researchers, we are not saying that valuing academic success is the only criterion of acting White. However, we are saying that it is one important criterion of acting White, and arguably the one criterion that may most be related to the actual academic achievement of African American students. Fordham seems to be suggesting that unless we include every possible criterion of acting White in a quantitative study, we are not really studying the phenomenon at all. There is a middle ground solution that I think is workable. Quantitative researchers should clarify that they are not studying the entire universe of attitudes and behaviors that could be considered as criteria of acting White, but rather select examples of these criteria. Furthermore, I think it would be fair to expect quantitative researchers to provide a rationale for why they are examining a certain criterion (e.g., valuing academic success) as opposed to another criterion (e.g., speech patterns, friendships, relationships, dress, etc.).

It is perhaps no coincidence that the empirical work of Karolyn Tyson and colleagues that I favorably reviewed earlier is the same empirical work that Fordham is specifically critical of. She dismissively characterizes Tyson et al. as arguing that the problem of acting White is not a Black thing. In fairness to Tyson et al., I believe that Fordham has oversimplified Tyson et al.'s arguments and, ironically, has misrepresented their findings. Tyson et al. do not simply say that acting White is not a Black thing. They say that the accusation of acting White is part of a larger general oppositional culture in which high-achieving

Black and White students are the targets of resentment for being perceived as arrogant. As mentioned earlier, for White students, this oppositional culture is class based; while for Black students, the oppositional culture sometimes becomes racialized (i.e., acting White). Disagreement with another scholar's work is no excuse for mischaracterizing or decontextualizing the scholar's work or for cavalierly dismissing the work without engaging the specific elements of the scholar's critique. Given Fordham's own legitimate concerns about how her work has been misread and mischaracterized, I would expect her to exercise more care in describing other scholars' work.

ANALYSIS AND CONCLUSIONS

This brief review of qualitative and quantitative studies regarding acting White and oppositional culture is not intended to be an exhaustive review of the literature. Indeed, there are many published and unpublished studies that have examined these themes among African American students. I have selected some of the more highly cited studies as exemplars of this body of literature. For example, the original Fordham and Ogbu study (1986) has been cited over 3,000 times. Bergin and Cooks (2002) has been cited over 120 times. While Harris (2011) is a relatively newer study and has been cited only approximately 20 times, it is published by Harvard University Press, and Angel Harris's scholarly profile as an authority in this area has steadily increased. Tyson et al.'s (2005) study has been cited almost 300 times, and is considered to be among the most comprehensive empirical studies of the topic. I spent considerable time analyzing and responding to Fordham's (2008) reflections. I believe that she has legitimate reasons to be concerned about how her work has been characterized, especially by media pundits who most likely have not even carefully read her work. I also agree with her analysis of sexist practices of male researchers. These sexist practices have resulted in the minimization of her central role in introducing the acting White thesis into the literature. I fear that I may have inadvertently contributed to her minimization, and thus I wanted to give Fordham her just due by devoting a significant amount of time to her ideas and reflections. While I agree with some of her observations, I have also pointed out some areas of disagreement.

So, what conclusions might be drawn about the acting White thesis? Anecdotally, it is very difficult to categorically dismiss it as an actual phenomenon. Every time that I have taught the Psychology of the African American Experience class (which has been around 20 times or so), I have had African American students share stories about being accused of acting White. In my own personal experiences, I can recall having cousins in Mississippi poking fun at me and telling me that I talked like a White person. It would be disingenuous to try to argue that the acting White phenomenon is nonexistent. However, the issue is not whether the acting White phenomenon exists or not. The real issue is whether the underachievement of African American students can be attributed to the burden or fear of acting White.

The empirical evidence is mixed on this question. Ironically, qualitative research, which according to Fordham would be most appropriate and most able to accurately capture acting White, is mixed in its support of the acting White thesis. For example, Fordham and Ogbu (1986) identified behaviors or attitudes associated with acting White that included spending a lot of time in the library studying and working hard to get good grades in school (among other non-school-related behaviors). They indicated that Black students who chose to pursue academic success were viewed as acting White by other Black students. *However, none of the quotes included from the students actually used the words acting White.* The acting White description was only used by Fordham and Ogbu to characterize the students' attitudes. In instances where they indicated that the students referred to acting White, no direct quotes were provided to help better understand the exact context. I want to be clear that I am not suggesting that there was a deliberate attempt to be misleading by Fordham and Ogbu. In fact, I think it was the exact opposite. I believe they (or maybe mostly Fordham) went into the research with the acting White thesis positioned to be the explanatory framework, and they conducted the research with this particular subjectivity. I am really expressing frustration at not being able to read direct quotes from students organically using the words acting White and in an unprompted manner. This is very frustrating to me, because it has not been my experience or observation that Black students would, without prompting, blame Black student underachievement on concerns of acting White. Interestingly, the word "brainiac" was used several times without prompting, which would seem to support Tyson et al.'s contention of a general oppositional culture.

Bergin and Cooks's qualitative study (2002) provides some evidence to support my concern. In their initial interview protocol, they did not specifically ask about acting White; instead, they asked a question about whether they had to give up their ethnic identity in order to do well in school. They pointed out that it became apparent that they needed to include a question that specifically asked about acting White. One can assume this was because none of the responses (or very few) included the words acting White. This is consistent with my concern that students only specifically mention acting White when prompted by a question. As I discussed earlier, the students were able to describe what was meant by acting White, and their descriptions covered a lot of themes that were not related to academics. One of their most significant findings was that students did not report avoiding academic achievement to avoid appearing to act White. While it certainly was annoying to some students (and somewhat amusing to others), the students were consistent in their attitudes that they would not allow the accusation of acting White to negatively impact their academic achievement.

Tyson et al.'s (2005) qualitative study did the best job of providing nuance on this issue by indicating that, based on their data, the burden of acting White was not a widespread phenomenon that negatively impacted academic achievement. They did acknowledge that in very specific circumstances, it *could* negatively impact academic achievement. They found the burden of acting White in only one out of eight schools where they conducted interviews. The following quote, in response to a question about whether friends had a reaction to this student being in AP and honors courses, was included as evidence of the burden of acting White:

> Oh man, they—a lot of people, well my good friends that are, that are in my honors English class, most of 'em, we take almost the same kinda course loads so I mean, we support each other. And then I have some other black friends that say I'm too smart, I'm trying to act white, or whatever, because I'm in such hard classes. (Tyson et al., 2005, p. 594)

Contrary to how Fordham (2008) characterized their study, Tyson et al. were actually very careful and nuanced in their analysis and conclusions. They did not categorically dismiss the idea of the burden of acting White. They only suggested that it was not a pervasive phenomenon among Black students and that there are similar underlying processes (i.e., oppositional culture) operating among high-achieving Black and White students.

Based on this review of the literature, I draw several conclusions about the acting White thesis. First, there are definitely some Black students who get accused of acting White. These accusations are sometimes in response to academic achievement, but are more often in response to other behaviors involving language, friendships, style of clothing, choice of music, etc. There are too many documented instances and anecdotes to deny its existence.

The second conclusion that I draw is that the burden or fear of acting White (relative to academic achievement) is not as widespread a phenomenon as the media, pundits, and politicians (yes, I am talking about President Obama) would have you believe. Empirical studies have simply not found this to be the case.

My third conclusion is that there is very little empirical evidence that supports the idea that the burden or fear of acting White actually undermines the academic achievement of Black students and is responsible for the achievement gap. Given the weak empirical evidence, efforts to close the achievement gap would be best served by not spending an inordinate amount of time addressing the burden or fear of acting White among Black students.

My fourth conclusion is that, contrary to conventional wisdom and popular belief, Black students do value school and education. Quantitative studies have repeatedly found that Black students do not devalue school, and that they tend to value school as much as White students. In spite of the problems that Fordham has with equating valuing school with acting White, I strongly believe that quantitative researchers should continue measuring how Black students value school.

In the next chapter I critically evaluate the arguments made by the African American linguistic scholar John McWhorter, in his book *Losing the Race: Self-Sabotage in Black America*. I closely examine his three major premises about Black culture. Specifically, I contend that McWhorter's book is irresponsible and that his premises about Black culture are remarkably naïve, insulting, and ignorant of relevant psychological and social science research.

4

Victimhood, Separatism, and Anti-Intellectualism: In Defense of Black Culture

In 2000, an African American linguistic scholar, John McWhorter, entered the public discourse on African American student achievement with the publication of his book *Losing the Race: Self-Sabotage in Black America*. McWhorter is characterized as offering "a daring assessment of what's plaguing the children of yesterday's affirmative-action babies." In the preface, McWhorter states his core belief that serves as the impetus for writing the book: the belief that "white racism is the main obstacle to black success and achievement is now all but obsolete" (McWhorter, 2000, p. x). Instead, McWhorter believes that the main reasons for the struggles of Black Americans are primarily ideological and psychological. McWhorter's argument was neither novel nor original. A decade earlier, Shelby Steele made essentially the same argument when he stated that Black students internalized a sense of inferiority that leads them to blame White people for their troubles and to form a victim's identity (Steele, 1990). Building on Steele's analysis, McWhorter provides a three-pronged argument that he argues is at the heart of Black students' academic underachievement. His argument consists of what he characterizes as three troubling ideological manifestations: "Cult of Victimology," "Cult of Separatism," and "Cult of Anti-Intellectualism."

CULT OF VICTIMOLOGY

McWhorter believes that Black Americans have been socialized to see themselves as victims of racism. This sense of victimhood has become a part of cultural Blackness and a core component of Black identity. He believes that Blacks fixate on racism so much that they are unable to acknowledge that racism is actually on the decline. He is careful to state that he is not arguing that there is no racism, only that racism is greatly diminished and not the problem that it once was. Furthermore, he argues that this sense of victimhood makes Black people hypersensitive to incidents that should not be seen as racist, or unable to objectively evaluate unflattering data about Black people without characterizing it as racist. Racism, he argues, does not explain everything, or even most things, related to the negative conditions of many Black people. Furthermore, he states that the majority of Black Americans live their lives largely unaffected by the dire portrayal of trenchant racism that is repeatedly perpetuated by Black scholars, politicians, and other influential individuals.

To support his argument, he provides several examples and anecdotes, which he states rather derisively as being real (as opposed to fictitious stories of racism provided by the late legal scholar Derrick Bell). Of the many examples and anecdotes he provides, a couple in particular are worth noting as they illustrate the problematic nature of his first argument. He recounts a story in which a Black undergraduate student at Stanford stated that her White mathematics professor told her to withdraw from a calculus class because Black people were not good at math. McWhorter indicates that he simply does not believe her. Is it because he possesses information that the student is lying? No. Is it because he possesses information that the student misunderstood what the professor said? No. Did he talk to the student and find her to be uncredible? No. He simply believed that the student is lying. Why? Because no White professor at an elite university such as Stanford in the late 1980s would dare make such a statement at the risk of damaging her reputation and career. So, because McWhorter could not possibly imagine that such a scenario would ever happen, he categorically dismisses the student's claim as an outright fabrication. The arrogance of McWhorter's statement is troubling, to say the least.

In the late 1990s, I was an assistant professor at Southern Illinois University at Carbondale. During one of our faculty meetings, we were doing student evaluations. One of my advisees, a Nigerian student, was having a lot of academic and clinical performance difficulties in the program. After an extended conversation about him, the training director stated if he didn't get his act together, his "Black ass" would be kicked out of the program. I will never forget that moment. I have never had a professional experience where I felt more like a persona non grata as much as I did at that moment in time. I remember looking around at my White colleagues and no one would make eye contact with me. I was in such shock that I was speechless and was emotionally disengaged from the rest of the meeting. As soon as the meeting was over, I left without saying a word and walked across campus to the Black Studies department. I found one of my colleagues and told her what happened. She asked me if I confronted the individual, and I told her that I was in such a state of shock that I did not say anything. She strongly communicated that I had to confront this individual, which I agreed had to happen. The next day I confronted her, and it appeared that she was anticipating the conversation. She immediately apologized and stated that as soon as she said it she knew it was inappropriate. I communicated how inappropriate her words were and how uncomfortable I had felt. Ultimately, I communicated that I was disappointed in her (especially given her own marginalized status as a lesbian). At the next faculty meeting she apologized and took responsibility for her inappropriate words.

Using the logic of McWhorter, one could say that I am lying and this experience did not happen to me. One might also say that no professor would ever say something so inappropriate, and arguably racist, about a student of color in a

faculty meeting. Well, I did not fabricate this story. It happened, and I had witnesses. But whether there were witnesses or not does not give McWhorter or
anyone else the right or authority to call me a liar without one shred of evidence
to support this character assassination. Yet this is exactly what McWhorter did
to this student. In his privileged and naïve world, learned White professors would
never say such things because they are simply too smart and concerned with self-
preservation to utter such offensive statements. This is probably the case for
many White professors who hold offensive beliefs, but to think that there would
never be an instance of this occurring is beyond naïve. It is intellectually lazy and
dishonest. Even a cursory review of the psychological literature on racial microaggressions would reveal this to not be the case. Often the racial microaggressions are more subtle than the experience I had or what was reported by the
African American student in McWhorter's anecdote. African American faculty
have reported (1) being asked questions about race from their White colleagues
that have no intellectual context but reflect assumptions that Black faculty are
the possessors of all knowledge related to Black people, or (2) being called "neu-
rotic" for trying to connect intellectual discussions to an African American context (Pittman, 2012). The racial microaggressions experienced by many African
American faculty should not be surprising given the research, which shows how
the authority and credibility of African American faculty is challenged by White
students (Harlow, 2003; McGowan, 2000; Pittman, 2010).

Racial microaggressions also occur in the form of resistance of White students
taking courses that address issues related to race and culture (Cokley, 2009;
Helms et al., 2003; Jackson, 1999). In their qualitative study of racial microaggressions against Black counseling and counseling psychology faculty, Constantine, Smith, Redington, and Owens (2008) identified several themes reported
by Black faculty, including (1) feeling marginalized/invisible as well as hypervi-
sible, (2) having qualifications challenged by faculty, students, and staff,
(3) expectations to serve on service-oriented roles with low perceived value,
(4) difficulties determining whether discrimination was related to race or gender,
(5) self-consciousness regarding choice of clothing, hairstyle, or manner of
speech, and (6) coping strategies to address racial microaggressions. Most salient
for my critique of McWhorter is the last theme. Among the strategies reported
by Black faculty were interpersonal or emotional withdrawal from faculty perceived to exhibit racial microaggressions, and resignation that racist treatment
will always exist in academia.

McWhorter is essentially trying to provide an analysis and commentary about
the psychology of Black people without either (a) having an understanding of
psychology, or (b) being knowledgeable about psychological and other social science research that would be relevant to the arguments that he makes. McWhorter's argument relies on the premise that Black students and faculty are essentially
hypersensitive to racism, seeing racism where it does not exist, and exaggerating

the frequency and intensity of racist experiences because that is part of the cult of victimology ideology that has become a core part of Black (American) identity. The amount of social science research that challenges McWhorter's premise is overwhelming. Nevertheless, it is from this assumption and its supposed resultant cult of victimology that the next prong of his argument, the cult of separatism, is presented.

CULT OF SEPARATISM

According to McWhorter, the cult of separatism is the direct result of the cult of victimology. He defines separatism as "the sense that to be black is to restrict one's full commitment to black-oriented culture and to be subject to different rules of argumentation and morality" (McWhorter, 2000, p. 72). Stated another way, McWhorter is referring to the idea that Black Americans always see Whites as hostile and White culture as being inimical to Black culture, and thus Black people need to be separate from White people and White culture in every way possible. McWhorter says that the cult of separatism is manifested in three ways: (1) mainstream culture as White culture, (2) the ghettoization of academic work, and (3) the belief that Black people can do no wrong.

Regarding mainstream culture as White culture, McWhorter argues that Black Americans are largely averse to expressions of mainstream culture because these expressions are seen as White culture. Because of this, Black people supposedly will not read novels by non-Black authors, listen to music by non-Black musicians, do research on non-Black issues, or learn foreign languages that are not spoken by Black people. McWhorter sees these personal preferences by many Black people as a problem that ultimately limits the experiences and career opportunities for Black people. On the surface, it is difficult to argue with what appears to be rather sound logic. As psychological research has shown, individuals who are more open to experience are generally more creative (Leung & Chiu, 2008) and exhibit less prejudice (Flynn, 2005; Sibley & Duckitt, 2008). However, if one considers openness to experience as a dimension of personality, as psychologists do, openness to experience is often linked more to political ideology (Carney, Jost, Gosling, & Potter, 2008; Sibley, Osborne, & Duckitt, 2012) than to what might be characterized as favorable outcomes.

Thus my critique of McWhorter on this aspect of his argument is primarily because of two concerns. First, as related to my primary interests in Black academic achievement and McWhorter's concern about Black academic underachievement, openness to experience actually has a very weak correlation with academic achievement, according to a recent meta-analysis (McAbee & Oswald, 2013). So, Black people can choose to have "narrowly" defined Black interests and have it not be linked to their performance in the classroom and overall academic achievement. My second concern is that White people have had narrowly defined interests for as long as the academy has been in existence; yet, there is no diminishment of their academic achievement, nor does McWhorter offer a critique of their narrowly defined "White" interests.

McWhorter goes on to characterize much of the work done by Black academics as ghettoized and minimizing logical argument and factual evidence because of a desire to essentially mythologize and idealize the Black present and past. He targets the intellectual paradigm of Afrocentricity and Afrocentric history, and cites as a primary example claims made about "Mother Egypt." He categorically dismisses Afrocentric claims as "primarily founded upon a fragile assemblage of misreadings of classical texts to construct a scenario under which Ancient Egypt was a Black civilization. . . . who therefore owed all notable culture to them" (McWhorter, 2000, p. 54). It is certainly true that some of the claims made by certain proponents of Afrocentric history are exaggerated, have little supporting evidence, are empirically unsound, and perhaps border on the incredulous. For example, the popular Afrocentric claim that Cleopatra was Black is dubious because it is based largely on flawed evidence from J. A. Rogers (1996, originally published 1946).

However, as evidenced throughout the book, McWhorter assumes that he can speak authoritatively about a topic for which he is intellectually and disciplinarily ill equipped to substantially address. For example, he belittles much of this work as another manifestation of the perpetuation of victimhood for the purpose of raising Black self-esteem. This cavalier and dismissive attitude is, I would argue, itself anti-intellectual because it does not engage the very serious research of the multitalented, interdisciplinary Senegalese scholar Cheik Anta Diop (e.g., Diop, 1974). Diop, who along with the Congolese scholar Theophile Obenga, provided very compelling (although disputed) evidence at the 1974 UNESCO (United Nations Educational, Scientific and Cultural Organization) Conference that the ancient Egyptians were Black. The hallmark of the academy is the ebb and flow of ideas that are supported through evidence and argumentation or refuted by the same. Scholars such as Diop are to be treated seriously, whether one agrees with him or not, and Black academics and students who are influenced by his scholarship should not be cavalierly dismissed as simply needing to believe in poor scholarship to boost their self-esteem. This attitude is arrogant and not befitting of someone who claims to be a scholar and intellectual.

There is another implication of McWhorter's characterization that is worth noting. The idea that much of the work of Black academics is ghettoized and lacking in logical argumentation is a not-so-slippery slope away from questioning the intelligence and methodological rigor of Black academics. While I am not suggesting that there are no examples of work by some Black academics that is underwhelming and not intellectually rigorous, the same observation can be made about any academic from any racial or ethnic background. There are academics who are White, Asian, Latino, Native, and other backgrounds whose research and scholarship is subpar, and it is not related to their racial or ethnic heritage. The fact of the matter is that much of the work done by scholars of color that focuses on issues of race, ethnicity, and culture is marginalized and not respected in the academy. This attitude is deeply embedded within the culture of the academy, and penalizes "minority" scholars whose methodologies and scholarship fall outside of the realm of what is considered to be important, rigorous mainstream research.

This issue is very personal for me because of my recent experience with being promoted to full professor. I have a joint appointment in the Department of Educational Psychology and the Department of African and African Diaspora Studies; thus, I had to go through two separate but concurrent reviews for promotion. In the Department of Educational Psychology, I received a unanimous vote at the department level. I also received a unanimous vote at the College of Education level. In the Department of African and African Diaspora Studies, I also received a unanimous vote at the department level. However, at the College of Liberal Arts level, the vote was 8 for promotion, 12 against. It was apparently one of the most contentious cases evaluated. The dean of the college disagreed with the decision, overturned it, and ultimately recommended that I be promoted.

In my debriefing with him, he communicated that he thought I had a strong case; thus, he was surprised at the nature of the comments and critiques made about me. There were two primary areas of critique leveled against me. First, there were criticisms about the methodology I use in my research. Specifically, the criticism was that I did not conduct experimental research. My research is primarily correlational, and uses a range of intermediate to advanced statistical analyses (e.g., regressions, canonical correlation, factor analysis, confirmatory factor analysis, and path analysis). The commentary being made was that my research methods were very basic and not sophisticated (i.e., no experimental manipulation). No consideration was made regarding whether the methods were appropriate for the types of research questions that I was asking, or were consistent with my particular training in counseling psychology. Additionally, no consideration was made that the overwhelming majority of racial or ethnic minority research in psychology does not use experimental research.

Another criticism was that I did not publish in enough "high impact" journals, and that I was publishing too much in niche journals (e.g., Journal of Black Psychology). This was a curious criticism, considering that I had published in the Journal of Black Psychology *only once during my time in rank as an associate professor (prior to being at the University of Texas, with an additional article in press). However, I did have one article published in the* Journal of Black Studies *(remember, I had a joint appointment in Educational Psychology and African and African Diaspora Studies). If the concern was about my ability to publish in top-tier, high-impact journals, then the fact that I was recognized as one of the top contributors to the* Journal of Counseling Psychology *between 1999 and 2009 should have assuaged that concern. I believe the real issue is that the individuals not supportive of my case thought that I had not published enough in top-tier, high-impact journals (which also means that they did not consider niche journals such as the* Journal of Multicultural Counseling and Development, Mental Health, Religion and Culture, Journal of Religion and Health, Journal of Diversity in Higher Education, *and* Cultural Diversity and Ethnic Minority Psychology) *as important or impactful outlets for scholarship. The dean, understandably, did not want to acknowledge that some larger force of systemic bias may have contributed to the negative evaluations of my case; yet he appeared to be genuinely perplexed and was unable to explain the outcome of my case.*

McWhorter's characterization of much of Black academics' work being ghettoized and lacking in logical argumentation is essentially the mind-set that contributed to the negative evaluation of my case, as well as the cases of so many Black faculty (and other faculty of color). Rather than carefully evaluating the specific theories, methodologies, analyses, and interpretations offered by a representative sampling of diverse Black scholars, McWhorter provides a broad, sweeping indictment of Black academics that makes for good tabloid journalism, but ultimately poor scholarship.

CULT OF ANTI-INTELLECTUALISM

McWhorter's diatribe on Black culture culminates with the third troubling ideological manifestation that he calls the Cult of Anti-Intellectualism. He characterizes this cult of anti-intellectualism as an internal, cultural trait that devalues learning. To set the tone for his chapter, he provides the following quote from an undergraduate Black student recruiter: "We're afraid that Black students who perform at that high a level aren't going to be concerned with nurturing an African-American presence at Berkeley" (p. 82). It is tempting to employ McWhorter's own tactics and simply dismiss this statement as never occurring. After all, he does not provide an actual name of the recruiter, which would at least give us the opportunity to contact the individual and verify the statement. One could make the argument that it would be easy to make up statements and incidents that cannot be documented for the sole purpose of increasing book sales. Because doing so would risk looking petty, I will not employ that tactic and will give McWhorter the benefit of the doubt that this statement was actually made. McWhorter obviously sees the statement as a perfect example of the supposed cult of anti-intellectualism. When I read the statement, I hypothesize that it is based on the recruiter's previous experiences with specific African American students who have perhaps excelled academically yet chose to not be involved in the African American community. The statement is impolitic, but it underscores an important concern regarding the importance of building a sense of community on a campus with a very small African American presence.

*It reminds me of an incident that occurred when I was an undergraduate student at
Wake Forest University. There was an academic scholarship for minority students,
and a biracial student had applied for it. As the story is told, the director of minority
affairs (who was responsible for choosing the recipients of the fellowship), met with
the student and essentially asked him whether he was going to be Black or White during
his time at Wake Forest. The director apparently was concerned about increasing the
numbers of African American students on campus, and did not want to "waste" a
scholarship on someone who was not going to be strongly identified as an ethnic minority
on campus. The student's parents apparently were very upset by this, and after they
complained to the administration, the Director was fired. It is easy to scapegoat the
director and dismiss his comments as problematic and inappropriate. To be sure, the
comments were politically unwise, to put it mildly. However, his concern was legitimate, and raises the larger question of whether a litmus test for racial identity should
be applied to individuals applying for "minority" scholarships. The short answer is obviously no, because it introduces additional problems (e.g.: Who makes the determination
of someone's "authentic" racial identity? What criteria will be used?). However, it
should be noted that the student received the award, was not involved with the Black
student community in any meaningful way, and, for all intents and purposes, primarily
socialized with White students.*

The point here is that McWhorter starts the chapter with this quote as
though it is prima facie evidence of anti-intellectualism in Black culture, when
a more culturally astute analysis would see the motivation underlying the quote
being more about wanting academically strong Black students with strong Black
identities. However, as is often the case throughout the book, McWhorter
presents anecdotes with precious little data and even less understanding of the
psychology and culture of African Americans.

McWhorter goes on to characterize Black undergraduate students at Berkeley
as among the worst students on campus. He recounts several incidents involving
Black students and poor academic performances (e.g., inadequate honors thesis,
failing a midterm exam, difficulty in completing homework, failure to take a final
exam, inconsistent class attendance, extremely late class enrollment). While
acknowledging that he had White and Asian slackers, too, he noted that slack-
ing was the norm for Black students. Anticipating the criticism that the behaviors he observed were not specific or disproportionately present in one group,
McWhorter shared another experience that he believed would definitively support his premise. This experience involved his teaching a nearly all-White and
Asian and nearly all-Black version of two classes. One of the classes was the history of Black musical theater, while the other class dealt with pidgin and creole
languages, Haitian creole, and Jamaican patois. In the nearly all-White and
Asian history class, McWhorter characterized the class as a success. He said that
the students loved the class, wrote great papers, and kept in touch with him after
the class concluded. However, his characterization of the nearly all-Black class

was quite different. He said that attendance was terrible, the students were not engaged in the material, and the midterm grades were bad. He noted that in the class dealing with languages, no Black student ever utilized his office hours for help, while pointing out that a White student did. These experiences reminded him of other teaching and educational experiences where he claimed to have observed similar behaviors. He dismissed the possibility that something about him and his teaching could be turning the Black students off because the predominantly White and Asian class had, according to him, thoroughly enjoyed the class (his exact words were "eaten up the same lectures and material") (p. 96). He definitively states that anti-intellectualism is "a central component of black identity" and that "black students do not try as hard as other students" (p. 101).

In my recent Politics of Black Identity class, I lectured on John McWhorter and his provocative commentary on Black students. As expected, the students had very strong and mostly negative reactions to his analysis. I also showed a YouTube clip of McWhorter involved in a panel debate on affirmative action (he is against affirmative action based on race). Interestingly, the students' negative reactions were even more intensified after observing him on the video. They found McWhorter to be very condescending and indicated that it was no surprise to them that Black students would act in the ways he reported. The students did not like his personality at all, and indicated that they would not want to take a class from him.

To demonstrate his racial bonafides, McWhorter acknowledges that racism is real (although greatly exaggerated and not responsible for the poor academic achievement of Black students), and proceeds to share his experiences of racism. McWhorter argues that other groups (e.g., Jews and Chinese) have experienced tremendous racism, yet they are still expected to have high academic achievement; however, a Black student who is called "nigger," is racially profiled, and is treated unfairly by teachers is doomed to forever be low achieving. McWhorter expresses righteous indignation over this and believes this to be an example of society underestimating Black people. To further support his point about the exaggerated impact of racism, McWhorter cites research by Lawrence Steinberg, who found that Latino and Asian students reported the same levels of racial bias, yet Asian students still excel academically. McWhorter conveniently does not address why Latino students do not also excel academically.

Teacher Bias

McWhorter then turns his attention to teacher bias as a factor in African American student achievement. He contends that this is a flawed argument because African American students do not fare any better in schools with mostly or all Black teachers. However, McWhorter once again misses the point. First, there is evidence for an effect of teacher race on academic achievement. For example, research has found that Black students who have Black math teachers are more likely to enroll in advanced math classes (Klopfenstein, 2005). Cultural differences in teacher communication is also a factor in student achievement, where White teachers' communication styles and lowered expectations can negatively impact Black student achievement (Irvine, 1990).

Second, the real issue is not so much about the race of the teachers, but rather the expectations of the teachers. In this regard, the literature is unequivocal. Teacher expectations have been found to account for as much as 42% of the racial gap in abilities and grades (Wildhagen, 2012). The evidence for lowered teacher expectations of Black students is overwhelming. When Black students are labeled gifted, they can still be subjected to more discrimination (Rubovits & Maehr, 1973). Furthermore, even when Black students have similar levels of achievement to White and Asian students, they still encounter lower teacher expectations (McKown & Weinstein, 2008).

While Black teachers are not immune from the prejudices of other teachers, research has also shown that Black teachers typically have higher expectations regarding academic achievement for Black students than White teachers (Beady & Hansell, 1981). There is also a strong gender bias, with teachers having lower expectations for independent and nonsubmissive Black males when compared to Black females (Ross & Jackson, 1991). While Black teachers typically have higher expectations for Black students, they are not immune from racial biases against Black students. Studies have also found no differences between Black and White teachers when making referrals for special education placement (Bahr, Fuchs, Stecker, & Fuchs, 1991). Empirical research has supported the idea that teacher bias can contribute to the Black-White test score gap (Ferguson, 2003). Differences in perceptions of teacher bias have been found to negatively impact academic achievement (Thomas, Caldwell, Faison, & Jackson, 2009). To argue that teacher racial bias is minimal and inconsequential is very naïve. It is nothing short of willful ignorance, and coming from an African American scholar who considers himself to be a public intellectual is the epitome of intellectual irresponsibility.

To further drive home his point about the minimal consequences of racism, McWhorter points out that children of Black African and Caribbean immigrants typically do better than Black Americans, although they are subjected to the same degree of racism. He cites Abner Louima, the Haitian immigrant who was assaulted and brutally sodomized with the handle of a plunger by New York police officers, and Amadou Diallo, the Guinean immigrant who was shot 41 times and killed by New York police officers, as examples of Black immigrants who experienced the harshest forms of racism. His logic is essentially that Black Africans and Caribbeans experience similar degrees of racism, yet Caribbeans still value school more and make better grades. McWhorter assumes that the experience of racial discrimination impacts Black Americans and children of

Black African and Caribbean immigrants similarly. However, research has shown that racial discrimination may differentially impact groups of African descent. For example, one study found that racial discrimination is negatively related to academic curiosity, persistence, and grades of Black American students (Neblett, Philip, Cogburn, & Sellers, 2006). Of course, McWhorter does not know (or take the time to research) empirical studies on this issue. He offers neither historical analysis nor empirical data to support his assumption, both of which are important for providing a context to understand the potential differential effects of racial discrimination.

A cursory examination of the literature reveals possible reasons for the differential outcomes. One study found that more frequent race-based experiences of discrimination was associated with higher anxiety for Black Americans but lower anxiety for Black Caribbeans (Soto, Dawson-Andoh, & BeLue, 2011). The authors propose that the resilience of Black Caribbeans may be attributed to a "healthy immigrant" effect where voluntary immigrants tend to be better adjusted among minority populations. Additionally, the processes of racial socialization differ across Black ethnic groups. Black American parents tend to emphasize racial discrimination more, while Black Caribbean youth may be less aware of racial discrimination because their parents minimize the impact racial discrimination has on upward mobility (Seaton, Caldwell, Sellers, & Jackson, 2010; Vickerman, 2001). While there may arguably be academic benefits to de-emphasizing racial discrimination, it can also result in diminished mental health (Seaton, Caldwell, Sellers, & Jackson, 2008).

Stereotype Threat

McWhorter moves on to cite Claude Steele's research on stereotype threat. He acknowledges that stereotype threat, or the fear that one will confirm negative stereotypes associated with one's social identity (e.g., race, gender, etc.), may undermine one's confidence. However, he summarily dismisses the idea that stereotype threat plays a significant role in the underachievement of Black students. He argues that other groups suffer from stereotypes (e.g., Vietnamese immigrants and being teased because of language and size), yet they still manage to excel in school. Essentially, McWhorter believes that to cite stereotype threat as a major factor in the underachievement of Black students is yet another manifestation of the cult of victimhood. Once again, McWhorter offers a selective, self-serving, and superficial reading of the empirical literature. No serious scholar that I am aware of has argued that stereotype threat is the major factor that accounts for Black underachievement. In fact, Claude Steele himself, in response to a similar criticism made by Arthur Whaley (1998), stated that stereotype threat is not the only threat to Black students disidentifying with academics (Steele, 1998). Steele also stated that factors such as poorly resourced neighborhoods, limited family resources, poor schools and teaching, and peers who are not invested in school all can undermine a Black student's identification with school. However, as the title of Steele's rebuttal article indicates, "Stereotyping and Its Threat Are Real" (Steele, 1998). McWhorter's analysis fundamentally misses the mark on an important finding of Steele's research: when stereotype threat is removed, equally skilled Black students (matched on comparable academic abilities) performed just as well as equally skilled White students. It does not make one a "Victimologist" to read the results of this study (and other highly controlled, experimental studies) and to conclude that stereotype threat is real and is of consequence in the academic performance (as measured by standardized test scores) of Black students.

Underfunded Schools

McWhorter continues along his mission to debunk all legitimate explanations of Black underachievement by briefly discussing underfunded schools. I emphasize briefly because he dedicates an entire five paragraphs to an issue that has been the focus of countless empirical studies. In his "review" of the literature, he cites 1989–1990 National Center for Education Statistics to show that minority school districts received more school funding than predominantly White districts. He argues that federal funding has greatly increased for inner-city schools, yet there is no significant improvement in their academic performance. Furthermore, he states that disadvantaged children from poor Southeast Asian refugees can be found in these schools, yet they still manage to excel academically.

It is important to disentangle multiple issues brought up in McWhorter's example. Yes, it is true that some school reform efforts that increased funding have not always been successful in improving academic outcomes. Some of these efforts have failed to significantly improve academic performance (e.g., Gross, Booker, & Goldhaber, 2009). However, there is also evidence that supports the importance of increasing school funding to improve academic outcomes (Henry, Fortner, & Thompson, 2010). School funding is often associated with issues of racial and socioeconomic segregation, such that schools with predominantly White and middle- to upper-middle-class students typically receive more funding than students with predominantly Black, Brown, and working-class or poor students. Using data from over 14,000 students in more than 900 high schools from the 1988 National Education Longitudinal Survey, researchers found that the socioeconomic level of schools was just as impactful on achievement as students' own socioeconomic status (Rumberger & Palardy, 2005). This impact was found for both advantaged and disadvantaged students. McWhorter's minimization of the impact of school funding on school achievement is consistent with conservative arguments that increased funding has not resulted in significant improvement in achievement. Of course, disparities in school funding are often inextricably linked to race and socioeconomic status. Black students are also disproportionately likely to be of lower socioeconomic status, which research has consistently shown to be negatively related to achievement (Sirin, 2005). However, McWhorter conveniently ignores these facts and their implications. Education scholars have long argued that funding gaps contribute to poor school performance and lower academic achievement for Black students (Ladson-Billings, 2007).

Tracking in School

McWhorter then turns his attention to tracking in school. Tracking is the practice of placing students in courses of instruction based on achievement or perceived skill level. The practice of tracking heavily relies on the use of standardized tests. McWhorter argues that, contrary to popular belief, there is no racial bias in tracking. He references four studies that support the idea that teachers do not place students based on racial bias, but simply by their prior performance. The studies he cites are in peer-reviewed journals, so it would seem that he finally has credible data to support his position. However, part of the issue here is around semantics. While it may be the case that there is no conscious racial bias involved in tracking (which I contend is still debatable), there is no question that there are racial disparities in tracking. In an ethnographic study, Childers (2011) found that there was racial stratification across three curriculums, with African American and other students of color being overrepresented in the lowest-level general college preparatory courses while advanced placement (AP) and international baccalaureate (IB) classes served primarily White students. Childers found that there were four reasons why racial stratification existed: (1) students chose to take lower level courses; (2) students of color needed to be directly recruited to apply to AP and IB classes; (3) African American students who applied for AP and IB classes coincidentally happened to not have the skills or abilities to be successful; and (4) recommendations against enrollment were perceived by students to be rejection, and thus they perceived that they were not allowed to enroll. Childers noted how discourses around individual choice and colorblindness dominated her discussions with White administrators when the issue of racial stratification was raised. Her observations of racial stratification in curriculum, and the reluctance to discuss reasons for racial stratification, is presented here as an example of a common experience in schools across this country. McWhorter argues that there is no racial bias in tracking, yet it is hard to determine whether this is the case when White teachers and administrators remain silent on race, or when they use the language of individual choice to suggest that the students want to be in lower-level courses. What he fails to do is to provide a deeper analysis that would ask why teachers and administrators find it acceptable that such racial stratification exists. McWhorter's characterization of teachers placing students in certain classes based simply on prior performance reflects his naiveté (or ignorance) about the ways in which race influences teacher perceptions and evaluations of students' skills and abilities.

McWhorter also fails to consider the role of standardized tests in tracking. It has long been documented that the use of standardized tests disproportionately negatively impacts racial minorities (Helms, 1992; Jencks & Phillips, 1998; Valencia & Suzuki, 2000). While he briefly engages the work of Claude Steele on stereotype threat and its role in Black students' academic performance, he fails to consider the most important context of stereotype threat: performance on standardized tests. If the research surrounding stereotype threat is valid, and there are many studies suggesting that it is, race would clearly have a role in taking standardized tests used to make decisions about tracking. So whether there is racial bias in tracking or not, one can reasonably conclude that the use of standardized tests (where racial disparities in performance are well documented) will likely perpetuate racial stratification in curriculum.

Oppositional Culture

McWhorter's core argument—indeed, the premise of his entire book—is that Black American culture is primarily responsible for the lower grades and general academic underperformance of African American students. He emphasizes culture because he argues that it crosses socioeconomic status. Citing the work of Signithia Fordham and John Ogbu (reviewed in the previous chapter), McWhorter argues that even middle-class African American students exhibit anti-intellectual attitudes that are no different from their less affluent counterparts. According to McWhorter, oppositional culture is actually a misnomer, because it assumes that there is a culture of racism against which Black students are reacting. Given that McWhorter believes that the experience of racism is greatly exaggerated among Black people, it is no surprise that he would find the term oppositional culture to be misleading. He prefers the term "cultural disconnect" from learning, which he says is part of the fabric of Black American culture.

Parental Expectations

McWhorter next briefly turns his attention to parental expectations. He states that Black parents have lower expectations regarding grades than both White and Asian parents. He references a study finding that Black parents have lower academic expectations than White and Asian parents do. As evidence, he states that one study found that Asian students indicated that their parents would not tolerate any grade lower than an A-. Of course, McWhorter assumes that none of us can imagine any Black parent taking this position, and he appears to assume (without critically interrogating the issue) that the attitudes of Asian parents are optimal and conducive to well-being. In doing so, he is promoting the "model minority" stereotype and ignoring a whole body of literature that addresses the stress and negative mental health outcomes that often accompany high parental expectations in Asian American culture (Lee et al., 2009; Murphy-Shigematsu, Sein, Wakimoto, & Wang, 2012). For example, Ying et al. (2001) found that while Asian American students at Berkeley had higher GPAs than African American and Hispanic American students, they had significantly fewer numbers of cross-racial friends, which was related to a lower sense of overall competence.

While others such as Amy Chua (2011), author of *Battle Hymn of the Tiger Mother*, have made claims of Asian (specifically, Chinese) cultural superiority being attributable to factors such as higher parental expectations, scores of detractors have given critical to scathing commentary about the book and Chua's controversial parenting methods. This emphasis on high parental expectations, which is a component of the cultural values argument that suggests that Asians have higher academic achievement because of their cultural values, also ignores evidence that the emphasis on achievement may be a result of a pragmatic concern about blocked opportunities for upward mobility due to discrimination (Sue & Okazaki, 1990). The point here is that McWhorter unnecessarily compares Black students to Asian students, which only serves to pit ethnic minorities against each other and invariably results in Black culture looking deficient. However, according to data from the National Educational Longitudinal Study, African American parents (along with Hispanic and Asian parents), actually tend to hold higher educational aspirations than White parents (Cheng & Starks, 2002). It is interesting that McWhorter fails to cite studies like this which challenge or contradict his narrative of Black cultural deficiencies and anti-intellectualism.

College Graduation Rates

It is tempting to go through each chapter and page of McWhorter's book to challenge each of his major arguments and examples. Even his personal anecdotes and observations, which would seem to be unchallengeable because they represent his lived experiences, are problematic in that he offers narrow interpretations of what are invariably complex social phenomena and interactions. One of the best examples can be seen in his brief discussion of college graduation rates. According to McWhorter, the lower college graduation rates of Black students is attributable in large part because education is valued less in the Black community than in the White community. He makes this statement based not on a shred of empirical data, but rather on his own observations. He surmises that Black students simply do not see completing a college degree as a central part of their adult identity. Even the most cursory review of the psychological and educational literature would have challenged his conclusion and should have resulted in his making much more nuanced statements. Analyzing data from the 1988 National Education Longitudinal Study, Kao and Tienda (1998) found that Black females aspire to more schooling than their White counterparts. They also found that Black males in the 8th grade were similar in educational aspirations to White males, but by the 10th grade, their educational aspirations had dropped (like all student subgroups except Asians) more precipitously than White males. Educational aspirations are highly correlated with parental socioeconomic status, so it is probably not surprising that groups who tend to be lower in socioeconomic status (Blacks and Latinos) may have more diminished educational aspirations over time compared to their White and Asian counterparts.

ANALYSIS AND CONCLUSIONS

It is clear that McWhorter is not motivated by a dispassionate analysis of data. He is a classic example of someone who cherry-picks data that support his ideological stance, in this case his belief in widespread Black anti-intellectualism. His ability to honestly and accurately reflect the nuances and complexities of social science data is embarrassingly low, yet he clearly believes himself to be a sophisticated consumer of this research. Since McWhorter does not actually conduct these studies himself, nor take the time to actually research and read the results of studies that do not support his assumptions or conclusions, he would not know (or care) that such studies exist.

The sheer arrogance of McWhorter is exemplified by his belief that his conclusions are drawn based on empirical evidence, while opposing views are not based on empirical evidence. McWhorter has created a tautological argument that is irrefutable because he sees any disagreement with his stance as an example of the anti-intellectualism he states is endemic to Black culture. It is this type of attitude that calls into question McWhorter's ability to serve as a public intellectual (which is clearly what he considers himself to be). McWhorter is not interested in having a genuine debate because he is unwilling to acknowledge that there are opposing arguments and views that are legitimate and based on empirical evidence. He does not allow for genuine ideological and philosophical disagreement. He buttresses himself from critique throughout the book by anticipating opposing viewpoints and summarily dismissing them as further examples of the "stranglehold" of victimology, separatism, and anti-intellectualism. In McWhorter's world, one cannot disagree with his analysis without being part of a Black culture that he tries to wax so eloquently about. His position is arrogance of the highest order.

McWhorter's primary motivation for writing the book was his belief that White racism was no longer the primary obstacle to Black success and achievement. McWhorter simply refuses to believe that racism is really as bad as Black folks claim it to be. Dramatic racial inequities across virtually all life domains would, based on McWhorter's logic, be primarily due to the poor choices and cultural failings of Black people. However, social scientists have long recognized what Eduardo Bonilla-Silva (2003) has called "racism with racists." I would recommend that any doubters of the trenchant and institutional nature of racism and systematic discrimination read Michelle Alexander's excellent book *The New Jim Crow* (Alexander, 2010). Using a dizzying array of statistics, Alexander presents a stunning critique of the criminal justice system, showing that discriminatory policies and practices are responsible for creating a permanent Black underclass. McWhorter's contention that Black Americans suffer from a mindset of "victimology" because they have been socialized to see themselves as victims of racism completely ignores the statistical, empirical, and factual reality that Black Americans continue to be the victims of institutional discrimination.

Furthermore, his arrogance is underscored by the fact that his conclusions are not drawn on a single shred of empirical data that he has collected and analyzed. He has not conducted a single empirical study himself, yet he has the audacity to claim that social scientists who disagree with him are simply part of the cult of victimhood and separatism that he has so astutely identified. McWhorter's position is essentially that anyone who does not attribute the underachievement of Black students entirely or predominantly to a cultural trait of anti-intellectualism is in fact manifesting the victimhood mentality that he sees as a part of Black culture. Although McWhorter is unqualified as a researcher and scholar to offer serious analysis on the achievement of African American students, the influence and widespread publicity of his book singlehandedly made him into a public intellectual celebrity. Thus, I needed to address his work that validates the idea of Black cultural deficiencies and, using empirical data, undo the damage he has done. I recommend that McWhorter stick to the topics in which he actually has scholarly authority (e.g., linguistics), and leave analysis of Black academic achievement to those scholars who have actually conducted research in the area.

In the next chapter I examine the issue of grades and what they mean to African American students. Because African American students often detach their self-esteem and academic self-concept from their grades, their behaviors and attitudes might be mistakenly interpreted as anti-intellectual. I hope to provide some insight about the complicated psychology involving the meaning of grades for African American students.

5

Black Students and Academic Disidentification: Why Grades Do Not Tell the Entire Story

The year 2007 marked the 50th anniversary of the desegregation of Little Rock Central High School. To commemorate this historic event, the documentary *Little Rock Central High: 50 Years Later* was produced. The video, characterized as "provocative," "sobering," and "powerful" by various media outlets, examined the legacy of desegregation and some of the challenges that still face American education around the education of Black students. In one of the most sobering and sad scenes, a White teacher tells her students to raise their hand if they know someone in their family who has gone to jail. Most of the African American students raise their hands, with many laughing (perhaps because of how normative it was for them). She then asks how many of their friends have been killed. One female student says the following:

> My uncle. It was gang related. He got shot from his bathroom all the way to his front yard. And my other uncle was also killed. In front of a grocery store.

The teacher clarifies "For drugs?" to which the student indicated yes. The student went on to explain:

> And his cousin shot him. It was gang related.

Another male student shared the following:

> I had a brother to get um. . . . he was, it was in the middle of a drug deal, and um . . . and he was um tied, beaten and burnt to death.

The young male student said this with what almost appeared to be a half smile on his face (although I'm sure it was not a smile). The teacher, with her hand clutched to her chest, gasps "Oh my God! Oh my God!" She calls on another female student, Jessica, who stated the following:

> My friend that graduated from here last year this summer she was murdered in Southwest. Umm, she was stabbed multiple times. And he threw her in a dumpster.

Many of the Black students showcased in the documentary were clearly from poor and working-class families. Now juxtapose these previous responses to comments made by Brandon Love, who was the student body president and clearly from a more affluent family:

> It kind of bothers me that Black kids come to school and we just come to kind of chill whereas the White kids come to get an education. You know they go on to do great things in life.

Another African American student riding with Brandon in his car agreed and made these observations:

> "I believe that's true. . . . because Black people . . . All they wanna do is go to school, hangout, and play sports. I mean that's basically it."

The saddest story to me was about 18-year-old Antron Pearson. The viewers are introduced to Antron by his telling the interviewer that he has been kicked out of the house by his mother. Antron is an aspiring boxer who has completely dis-identified from school. At one point one of his teachers, Shannah Ellender, is talking to him about his missed classes and telling him that he cannot miss any more classes. Ten or more unexcused absences means Antron will have to repeat the grade. After Antron leaves the room, Ms. Ellender tells the interviewer the following:

> Antron, he can't read. He may read on a 3rd grade level. He's got a low F in Spanish 1. He's got a 16. Low F in Biology 1. He's got a 57 F in Drama. He has a zero in World History, F. Too many absences to pass the class at all. So he doesn't even have a shot at getting, at being able to pass these classes. Which means it's a waste of a semester. He'll have to retake all these classes which means he'll be a freshman a 9th grader again next year. And will be 18 years old.

Ms. Ellender goes on to talk about how depressing and frustrating it is because there are people trying to help Antron. The interviews with most of the White people show that there is a common belief that African American students do not work hard and do not value school. This belief is held not only by White people, as we see evidenced by the statements made by Brandon and his friend. The first few statements made by the students reveal young lives exposed to unspeakable violence. The nature, level, and frequency of violence disclosed by these young students make it perfectly understandable if their focus was less on school and more on survival.

In the case of Antron, he is an example of a student who has completely dis-identified from school. He clearly is not invested in school as evidenced by him failing every class. One might assume that given his extremely poor academic performance, he would have low self-esteem. However, the images that we see of him throughout the video tell a very different story. Antron is supremely confident in his boxing skills, and believes he is good enough to become a professional boxer one day. Judging how confident he appeared walking down the hall smiling and talking to students, Antron does not appear to suffer from low self-esteem. If anything, he appears to have high self-esteem, in spite of the fact that he is failing all his classes.

In this chapter, I examine the relationship between grades and self-esteem among African American students. In spite of lower grades, African American students maintain high self-esteem and academic self-concept. Stereotype threat is a phenomenon that involves a fear of confirming a stereotype in a domain, often academic, based on one's social identity (e.g., race or gender). Stereotype threat causes academic disidentification, which occurs when self-esteem becomes disconnected from academic achievement. Several reasons for academic disidentification are examined, including devaluing school and discounting academic feedback. I argue that academic disidentification is misunderstood as being a negative orientation to school and learning, and consequently contributes greatly to the perception of African American students being anti-intellectual.

SELF-ESTEEM

Self-esteem is one of the oldest topics in psychology and is a fundamental topic in the social sciences (Mruk, 2013). There are few outcomes where self-esteem is not implicated in some way. The most obvious implication of self-esteem involves mental health. For example, according to O'Brien, Bartoletti, and Leitzel (2006) (cited in Mruk, 2013), self-esteem is involved as a diagnostic criterion in almost 25 mental disorders listed in the *Diagnostic and Statistical Manual of Mental Disorders* (American Psychiatric Association, 2000). While many definitions for self-esteem exist, a useful definition that incorporates elements of different theoretical approaches is one's personal sense of competence and worthiness (Mruk, 2013).

Given the historical and contemporary experiences of racist oppression, it has long been assumed that African Americans would demonstrate lower self-esteem than European Americans. After all, if you are born into a world where you are constantly bombarded with messages about Black inferiority and Black people as problems, it seems reasonable to conclude that exposure to and internalization of those messages would result in African Americans having lower self-esteem. This assumption was seemingly supported by the early doll studies by Kenneth and Mamie Clark (Clark & Clark, 1947). These studies involved 253 Black children ranging in ages from 3 to 7. The purpose of the studies was to examine their preferences for a brown or white doll. In response to a request from the NAACP, the Clarks conducted an additional study at Scott's Branch Elementary School among 16 Black children between the ages of 6 and 9. The children were asked to respond to the following seven prompts:

1. Show me the doll that you like best or that you would like to play with
2. Show me the doll that is the nice doll
3. Show me the doll that looks bad
4. Give me the doll that looks like a white child
5. Give me the doll that looks like a colored child
6. Give me the doll that looks like a Negro child
7. Give me the doll that looks like you

The Clarks found that 10 out of the 16 children chose the white doll as the one they liked best and the one they considered a nice doll. Eleven of the 16 children chose the brown doll as the doll that looked bad. The Clarks indicated that these results were consistent with research they had conducted on over 300 children, and concluded that Black children had internalized feelings of inferiority and self-hatred as early as the age of 6. They attributed this "self-hatred" ultimately to the effects of segregation.

The Clark doll studies are among several studies that have sought to ostensibly measure Black self-esteem through the use of various external stimuli including dolls, drawings, and photographs (Banks, 1976). In fact, it was Curtis Banks, an African American psychologist and former editor-in-chief of the *Journal of Black Psychology*, along with Joseph Baldwin, a prominent Afrocentric psychologist, who provided two of the most astute critiques of the literature on White preference in Blacks phenomenon. In Banks's (1976) examination of this body of literature, he found that among 21 investigations of this phenomenon, 2 (9%) clearly found support of White preference among Blacks, 4 (19%) found support of Black preference among Blacks, while 15 (71%) found inconsistent preferences or no preferences at all. Baldwin's (1979) criticisms of the racial preference literature included (1) limited empirical support, (2) conceptual imprecision in constructs such as Black self-concept, (3) experimenter effects (i.e., race of experimenter-influenced responses of Black participants), (4) failure to determine what the choice meant to the children, (5) the likelihood that Black dolls prior to the 1960s were probably novel stimuli, and (6) the failure to consider that some Black children may not have understood the meaning of the evaluative tasks (Baldwin, 1979; Banks, 1976). An additional limitation of the doll studies (and indeed most of the racial preference literature) is that while conclusions about self-esteem and self-concept were drawn, these constructs were not typically ever explicitly measured. Ultimately, the conclusions of Black self-hatred drawn from the study were challenged by Black psychologists for conceptual, empirical, and methodological reasons.

The limitations of the doll studies notwithstanding, the power of Clark's research and testimony was pivotal in the Supreme Court ultimately ruling that segregation "generates a feeling of inferiority as to their status in the community that may affect the childrens' hearts and minds in a way unlikely ever to be undone" (*Brown v. Board of Education*, 1954). The racial preference studies were the foundation for thinking that Blacks collectively had low self-esteem, especially in comparison to Whites. However, two highly cited empirical studies challenge this assumption. In one study, Gray-Little and Hafdahl (2000) conducted a meta-analysis of studies involving 261 Black and White comparisons of self-esteem. They found that Black children, adolescents, and young adults on average had higher self-esteem than their White counterparts. While the statistical effect size is small, it is nonetheless a consistent and notable finding that goes against conventional wisdom and traditional psychological theorizing regarding self-esteem and social status. In trying to explain why Blacks do not have lower self-esteem, Gray-Little and Hafdahl suggest that the social referents for Blacks are not Whites, but rather other Blacks. In other words, the self-esteem of Blacks is based on how Blacks compare themselves to other Blacks rather than to Whites. Additionally, they suggest other reasons that Blacks have higher self-esteem. One reason is because of a desire to emphasize their distinctiveness as a social group, which becomes associated with individual self-esteem. Another reason is because ethnic/racial identity is more salient for Blacks than for Whites, and also has a stronger relationship with self-esteem for Blacks than for Whites. They also found that the Black self-esteem advantage increases with age, and was also larger for general self-esteem than academic self-esteem. The authors concluded that the role of academic achievement in academic self-esteem differs by race, implicating the process of academic disidentification.

In another meta-analysis, Twenge and Crocker (2002) replicated and extended Gray-Little and Hafdahl's (2000) study by examining race differences in self-esteem among 712 sources of data. Similar to Gray-Little and Hafdahl's study, Twenge and Crocker found that Blacks had higher self-esteem than Whites, and this self-esteem advantage increased over time for Blacks. Blacks also had higher self-esteem than Asian Americans and Latino/a Americans. Also similar to Gray-Little and Hafdahl (2000), Twenge and Crocker conclude that Black students are less likely to base their self-esteem on the opinions of other people. They recommend that researchers should stop examining questions about racial differences in self-esteem and instead ask which members of these groups have low or high self-esteem and why.

Based on these comprehensive reviews of the literature, it can be concluded that Black students do not exhibit a preference for Whites and do not suffer collectively from internalized racial self-hatred. Black students will typically exhibit

higher self-esteem than White students. Furthermore, it can be tentatively concluded that the basis of Black students' self-esteem will often be in comparison to
other Black students rather than White students.

ACADEMIC SELF-CONCEPT

A related construct to self-esteem is academic self-concept. Academic
self-concept is how confident a student feels about her or his academic abilities.
Academic self-concept is an important construct because it has consistently
been positively correlated with grades (Awad, 2007; Cokley, 2000; Lent, Brown,
& Gore, 1997; Marsh & Martin, 2011; Reynolds, 1988; Shavelson & Bolus,
1982) as well as self-esteem (Awad, 2007; Marsh & O'Mara, 2008; Witherspoon,
Speight, & Thomas, 1997). Furthermore, academic self-concept has been found
to have reciprocal effects on academic achievement and educational attainment,
while self-esteem has been found to have virtually no effects (Marsh & Craven,
2006; Marsh & O'Mara, 2008). Several studies have also examined racial/ethnic
differences in academic self-concept, with earlier studies finding that African
American students have higher academic self-concepts than their White peers
(Fulkerson, Furr, & Brown, 1983; Lay & Wakstein, 1985).

In a study comparing 159 French, 62 White, and 78 African American students in the seventh grade, Kurtz-Costes, Ehrlich, McCall, and Loridant (1995)
found that African American students had higher academic self-concepts than
both French and White students. Interestingly, African American students were
more likely to attribute their academic success to ability, while French and
White students were more likely to attribute their academic success to the
amount of effort they exerted.

In a large study involving over 12,000 adolescents, Martinez and Dukes
(1997) examined ethnic identity and academic self-concept. Not surprisingly,
Black and Hispanic students had the highest ethnic identity, followed by Asian
students. White and Native American students had the lowest ethnic identity.
The authors found that African American students had lower academic self-
concepts than White and Asian students, but higher academic self-concepts
than Hispanics and Native Americans. They also found that ethnic identity
was positively correlated with academic self-concept. This is also consistent with
more recent research that has found both ethnic and racial identity to be positively correlated with academic self-concept (Cokley & Chapman, 2008; Cokley
& Moore, 2007) and academic efficacy (Oyserman, Harrison, & Bybee, 2001).

Another study included approximately 1,500 African American and European American socioeconomically diverse students in elementary school to post-
secondary school (Eccleston, Smyth, & Lopoo, 2010). The authors found that
African American students had a more positive reading academic self-concept
than European American students, but were similar in math academic

self-concept. Consistent with the aforementioned meta-analyses, the authors also found that the overall self-esteem of African American students was more positive than that of European American students.

Using a nationally representative and racially diverse sample of approximately 7,000 students in grades 7–12, Lehman (2012) found that African American students reported the highest academic self-concept among Asian Americans, Hispanics, and Whites. Furthermore, among African American students, he found that perceptions of prejudice and racial diversity of friendships were negatively correlated with academic self-concept, while racially homogenous friendships (i.e., having mostly Black friends) was positively correlated with academic self-concept.

Findings regarding academic self-concept are generally consistent with findings about self-esteem. Studies typically report that African American students have higher academic self-concepts than White students.

STEREOTYPE THREAT

In one of the most highly cited articles related to the academic performance of African American students, Claude Steele and Joshua Aronson introduced the concept of stereotype threat (Steele & Aronson, 1995) into the academic literature, and later into the popular literature (Steele, 1999). Claude Steele had started work on stereotype threat among women during his time at Michigan and in collaboration with a graduate student, Steven Spencer (Steele, 2010). Later, after he moved to Stanford, he was joined by a postdoctoral student, Joshua Aronson, with whom he collaborated to apply stereotype threat to African American students. According to Steele and Aronson, stereotype threat is "being at risk of confirming, as self-characteristic, a negative stereotype about one's group" (Steele & Aronson, 1995, p. 797).

Steele and Aronson conducted a series of experimental studies to test the existence of stereotype threat. In the first study, 114 Black and White students were assigned to experimental and control groups and given a 30-minute test from the verbal GRE (with preexisting SAT differences being statistically controlled for). For the stereotype threat condition, students were told that the test represented a diagnostic test of ability. For the non-stereotype threat condition, the test was described as a laboratory problem-solving task. In the other non-stereotype threat condition, students were told that the test is a difficult challenge. The results indicated that Black students in the stereotype threat condition performed worse than Black students in both non-stereotype threat conditions, and also performed worse than White students in the stereotype threat condition. In essence, when the test was presented as a test of ability, Black students performed worse than White students; however, when it was presented as non-diagnostic of ability, Black students performed as well as White students.

In the second study, only Black and White female students participated. They took the same test, but it was offered on a computer and they had only 25 minutes (compared to the 30 minutes in the first study). The results were similar to the first study. In addition, the Black female students in the stereotype threat condition tended to respond more slowly to the test items than the Black female students in the non-diagnostic condition (94 seconds versus 71 seconds) and White female students in the stereotype threat condition (73 seconds) and non-diagnostic condition (71 seconds).

In the third study, they were interested in whether stereotype threat actually activated racial stereotypes in the thinking and information processing of Black students. Similar to the first two studies, students were placed in two conditions, one stereotype threat condition and one non-stereotype condition. Students engaged in a word fragment completion test, where 12 out of 80 word fragments had a race-related construct or an image associated with an African American as possible solutions. For example, "__ce" could be completed as "race," "la__" could be completed as "lazy," "__ack" could be completed as "black," and "__or" could be completed as "poor." Students were instructed to spend no more than 15 seconds on each item. Black students in the stereotype condition were more likely to complete the word fragment with a race-related construct than Black students in the non-stereotype condition and White students in the stereotype threat condition. Students were also told to rate their preferences for a range of activities, which included activities that are stereotypically associated with African Americans (e.g., rap music, basketball). Black students in the stereotype threat condition were also the least likely to prefer activities that were stereotypically associated with African Americans when compared to Black students in the non-stereotype threat condition and White students in both conditions.

Steele and Aronson concluded that the instructions clearly played a role in arousing stereotype threat among the Black students in the first three studies. In their fourth and final study, they examined whether identifying race would be enough to arouse stereotype threat. Once again, Black and White students were placed in a stereotype threat condition and non-stereotype threat condition. In the stereotype threat condition, the last item of the demographic sheet asked students to indicate their race, while students in the non-stereotype threat condition did not have to indicate their race. Students took the test on paper and were given 25 minutes. As hypothesized by the authors, Black students in the stereotype threat condition performed worse than Blacks in the non-stereotype threat condition and Whites in the stereotype threat condition.

From this final study, Steele and Aronson concluded that even when a test is not presented as diagnostic of ability, priming racial identity (i.e., making race salient by having students indicate their race) was still powerful enough to negatively impact Black students' performance. In trying to make sense of the findings, Steele and Aronson surmise that stereotype threat makes Black students less efficient in processing information. Students who were stereotype threatened "spent more time doing fewer items more inaccurately" (Steele & Aronson, 1995, p. 809). They suggest that it is precisely stereotype threat that leads students to academic disidentification.

In writing this section, I have tried to recount instances where I have observed stereotype threat and its effects. You would think that in 16 years of teaching, I should be able to easily recall instances where stereotype threat was present and negatively affected my African American students (or me, for that matter). However, I struggled to think of specific instances. I realized that the nice experimental conditions of the social psychology laboratory were not translating into easily identifiable experiences as I had anticipated. Then I realized that the experiences were perhaps more subtle and less dramatic than the examples provided by Steele's research.

For example, when I first started teaching as a professor, I was 29 years old. Given my age and the fact that I had recently completed my PhD, I was concerned about appearing to be competent to undergraduate and graduate students. On the one hand, this can be seen as a common concern among all newly minted PhDs who go straight to graduate school after graduating college. I tried to project an air of authority and competence by wearing a coat and tie to school every day that I taught a class. However, I was also very concerned about how I communicated in class. I was extra attentive to the way that I talked, making sure that I was not violating any grammar rules (e.g., subject/verb agreement), not using Ebonics, and pronouncing words correctly. I was also very concerned about being able to answer questions correctly. These concerns took on a decidedly racial overtone because I did not want to be perceived as an incompetent and unqualified Black professor. I felt that I was "representing the race," so I needed to always speak properly and answer all questions correctly. On the occasion that I would misspeak, I never thought of it as simply students seeing me as an individual making a mistake. Instead, I always believed that students (especially White students) were judging me as less intelligent and seeing me as a product of affirmative action. In my mind, this is another manifestation of stereotype threat. While research studies have typically included a prompt that made race more salient (e.g., instructions regarding tests of ability or demographic forms indicating race), I believe that Steele (1997) was accurate in describing stereotype threat as "a threat in the air." In my case, and I suspect in the cases of many African American students, there did not need to be an explicit prompt to make race salient for me. Did this awareness or concern about race cause me to misspeak? According to the logic of stereotype threat, probably yes. I am less certain that this is the case; however, I am certain that I was concerned about not perpetuating racial stereotypes related to Blacks being less intelligent. Whether these types of preoccupations disrupt or undermine academic performance is a question for researchers to continue to examine. However, there is no doubt in my mind that stereotype threat is a part of the psychological apparatus or makeup of African American students that is important to understand.

There have been hundreds of published studies and dissertations on stereotype threat, with its effects having been well documented in the literature. Stereotype threat has been linked to high blood pressure (Blascovich, Spencer, Quinn, & Steele, 2001), lowered test performance (Steele & Aronson, 1995), lowered academic learning (Taylor & Walton, 2011), and impaired problem-solving (Carr & Steele, 2009) among Blacks; racial distancing behavior among Whites (Goff, Steele, & Davies, 2008); and aggression, unhealthy eating, and risky decision making among women (Inzlicht & Kang, 2010). The specific mechanisms that explain why stereotype threat disrupts academic performance include (a) a physiological stress response that impairs cognitive processing, (b) a tendency to actively monitor performance, and (c) attempts to regulate and suppress negative thoughts and emotions (Schmader, Johns, & Forbes, 2008). Among the domains in which stereotype threat is believed to have an impact, attitudes toward school is most directly implicated in the characterization of Black students being anti-intellectual and not valuing school because of the process of academic disidentification.

ACADEMIC DISIDENTIFICATION

According to Steele, one of the consequences of stereotype threat is disidentification with school, a concept first introduced in the literature by Jeremy Finn's discussion of school withdrawal and the failure of students to develop a sense of identification with school (1989). In fact, prior to introducing the idea of stereotype threat to the public, Claude Steele introduced the concept of academic disidentification in the *Atlantic Monthly* (Steele, 1992). In this article, Steele started off by briefly reviewing the litany of statistics and data that illustrate Black underachievement: lower grades at every grade level, higher dropout rate at every grade level, and a decrease in the number of PhDs awarded. Steele then briefly reviewed the common set of explanations used to explain Black underachievement. One by one, he rejected each explanation as being inadequate. Regarding socioeconomic status, where it is well documented that socioeconomic status is correlated with academic achievement (Sirin, 2005; White, 1982), Steele indicated that even middle-class Black students at wealthy schools still underperform compared to middle-class White students at the same schools. He also ruled out skills deficits, because even when Black students have comparable SAT scores (which he equates with measuring academic skills), they still underperform academically in comparison to White students. In addition, he ruled out the argument that Black American culture simply does not value education by pointing out that the results of many surveys indicate that Black students do value education highly, and often more than White students. Steele believed that while each of these explanations partially explain Black underachievement, each involved limitations. He believed that there was still something else involved.

He finally settled on a social psychological explanation that he called academic disidentification. Steele characterized disidentification as the process wherein self-esteem becomes disconnected from academic achievement. Years before the label of academic disidentification was applied to African American students, studies had reported that Black students were more likely to disconnect their self-esteem from academic achievement in comparison to White students (Demo & Parker, 1987; Rosenberg & Simmons, 1972). To illustrate, Steele talked about his own graduate school experience where he conducted experiments with his advisor. He did the work because he wanted a PhD, but he acknowledged that he was not necessarily excited about the work and he had not fully internalized a social psychologist identity. However, over time, he began to gradually like the work, and he became genuinely excited about it. His excitement manifested in ways such as meeting deadlines, constantly wanting to talk about arcane theories, and becoming emotionally invested in the outcomes of his experiments. Steele indicated that these academic and intellectual activities were becoming a part of his self-esteem. In other words, he was becoming increasingly identified with academics. According to Steele, one overlooked factor in his becoming identified with academics was being treated as a valued person with good potential and constant reaffirmation.

I am reminded of a recent intervention involving African American doctoral students in a graduate program. Everywhere that I have taught, ethnic minority students have eventually come to me to discuss their experiences in their graduate programs. I am not remarkable in this regard, as I believe this often happens with faculty of color who care about ethnic minority students. I addressed a group of faculty about my concerns regarding the experiences of African American students. The students had reported a series of negative incidents and racial microaggressions that was making their graduate experience very difficult, if not miserable. The students reported several overlapping concerns including lack of research opportunities, feeling invisible, feeling less invested in than their White peers, and not feeling supported or cared for. These concerns alone are difficult and would be enough to facilitate students becoming disidentified from their graduate studies. However, what made these students' experiences even more intolerable were their experiences of racial microaggressions. One student reported that during a presentation, a student supported early childhood programs that would take African American babies away from their families and place them with White families because research showed that White structure is better. The African American student indicated that she became very heated and argued from a researcher's perspective with the offending student. She characterized the professor as not saying much at all, and then during the break, asking a question regarding how she felt about Obama being elected as president. The student reported being nearly in tears from the sense of rage that she felt. Another incident was reported in which a student made the comment that if African American students did not listen to music, play sports, and dance so much, they would perform better on IQ tests. The professor did not respond (although he indicated afterward to me that he literally did not hear the comment because of his poor hearing). These types of incidents set a tone for a racially hostile and unsupportive climate that contributes to academically strong and successful African American students becoming increasingly disengaged from school. Indeed, what led me to eventually initiate a discussion with these faculty were my observations of confident African American students slowly and systematically being broken down, becoming discouraged, and questioning their career goals. I was literally watching African American students go through the process of academic disidentification, and I had reached the point where I wanted to express to this particular graduate program that they should no longer accept African American students given their poor treatment. I knew that when I began to feel this way, I needed to address these faculty.

Steele continues by describing what he calls racial devaluation, which he says terms like prejudice and racism do not fully capture. He gave examples of the ways in which Black people are racially devalued—not so much by overt racism, which of course happens, but rather by more subtle acts including lack of Black images in advertising, failure to see Black women as romantic partners in the media, lack of Black representation in school curricula, and lack of acknowledgment of Black literary and musical canons. Racial devaluation can be also seen in the failure of well-intentioned teachers to acknowledge the talents and potential of Black students at a time when the students care very much about the academic domain. The constant bombardment of these images and messages, Steele argues, is a source of racial devaluation. The end result is a Black student who, consciously or unconsciously, disidentifies from school by separating his self-esteem from academic endeavors.

Steele's introduction of academic disidentification into mainstream discourse via the *Atlantic Monthly* has prompted several studies of the phenomenon. One of the earliest studies was conducted by Jason Osborne (1995). Using data from the National Education Longitudinal Study, Osborne examined Steele's disidentification hypothesis that self-esteem is more likely to become detached from academic achievement among African American students than among White students. For the purposes of his study, Osborne used a sample of 8th- and 10th-grade students that consisted of 544 African American male students, 689 African American female students, 5,294 White male students, and 5,473 White female students. Osborne then tested each assumption of Steele's (1992) theory of academic disidentification. First, there were differences in academic achievement, with African American students scoring lower on the measures of academic achievement than White students. Next, African American students in both 8th and 10th grades had higher self-esteem than White students. Finally, between the 8th and 10th grades, the correlation between self-esteem and GPA scores significantly decreased for African American males, increased (but not significantly) for White males, and decreased (but not significantly) for African American males, while showing largely no change for White females.

Among the most cited academic disidentification studies is another study conducted by Osborne (1997). Using the same data from the National Educational Longitudinal Study, Osborne included African American, Hispanic, and White samples with data collected in 1988, 1990, and 1992. Once again, testing Steele's (1992) disidentification hypothesis, differences were found in academic achievement, with White students reporting higher grades than African American and Hispanic students at all three time points. Grades remained stable for White students at all three time points, while decreasing for Hispanics and especially so for African Americans. Consistent with previous research on self-esteem, African Americans had higher self-esteem than Whites and Hispanics across all three time points. Osborne points out that while the self-esteem of African Americans remained higher than Whites, over time their grades and achievement scores were decreasing. When the disidentification hypothesis was examined using self-esteem and achievement scores, the correlations decreased most significantly for African American boys followed by African American girls. The only other group for which disidentification was present was among Hispanic boys between the 10th and 12th grades. When the disidentification hypothesis was examined using self-esteem and grades, African American boys once again demonstrated the most dramatic decrease over time. All other groups also demonstrated decreases over time, although Hispanic and White girls had a modest increase at the 2nd time point followed by a slight decrease at the 3rd time point. Osborne points out that it is interesting that these gender differences emerge regarding African American males because Steele did not hypothesize that gender differences would exist.

Using a small sample of 96 African American high school students, I was interested in examining academic disidentification in terms of both (a) the relationship of academic self-concept to GPA, and (b) variables related to academic disidentification being used to predict GPA (Cokley, McClain, Jones, & Johnson, 2011). I found evidence of disidentification among African American males, where the correlation between academic self-concept and GPA significantly decreased from younger males (< 17.33 years old) to older males (> 17.33 years old). However, among African American females, there was evidence of stronger identification with school as evidenced by a statistically significant increase in the correlation between academic self-concept and GPA between younger females and older females. Additional evidence of disidentification was found by gender and age both being predictors of GPA. Females had higher GPAs than males and age was a significant negative predictor of GPA, suggesting that as students get older, they become more disidentified with school.

Radziwon (2003) examined 8th-grade students' identification with school. His sample included approximately 3,300 students, of which over 800 were African American students. Identification with school was measured using two subscales: belonging (i.e., how much a student feels connected to the school) and valuing (i.e., a student's belief in how useful are the knowledge and skills learned in school). African American students reported higher levels of identification with school than White students.

Generally when academic disidentification is discussed, it is within the context of students in middle school and high school. It is often assumed that students in college would not experience academic disidentification because there is usually a certain amount of motivation and presumably identification with school that is required to be a college student. I tested this assumption by examining academic disidentification in a group of college students (Cokley, 2002a). In this study I had a sample of 358 African American students and 229 White college students. Similar to Osborne (1995), I proceeded to test Steele's theory of academic disidentification. African American students had significantly lower grades than White students, which met the first assumption of Steele's hypothesis. However, African American students reported significantly higher self-esteem than White students, which met the second assumption of Steele's hypothesis. I also tested whether African American students would have higher academic self-concept than White students, which, while not explicitly theorized by Steele, would still be consistent with his theory. African American students did report significantly higher academic self-concept than White students. Dividing the sample between underclassmen and upperclassmen, there was evidence of disidentification among African Americans with a decrease in the correlation between academic self-concept and GPA; while White students demonstrated an increase in the correlation between academic self-concept and GPA. Interestingly, using self-esteem, there was no evidence of academic identification for either African American or White students.

Based on Osborne's findings of gender differences, I disaggregated the data by gender. Similar to Osborne, I found the strongest evidence of disidentification among African American males. African American females and White males had slight decreases in the correlation between academic self-concept and GPA; however, there was still a statistically significant positive relationship for both underclassmen and upperclassmen. White female underclassmen had a nonsignificant relationship between academic self-concept and GPA, but White female upperclassmen had the largest and strongest positive relationship. On the other hand, among African American males, the correlation was positive and statistically significant among underclassmen, but not statistically significant among upperclassmen. Using self-esteem, there was evidence of academic disidentification among all groups except for White females, for whom there was evidence of an increased identification with academics.

I have witnessed firsthand how academic disidentification is most pronounced among African American males. Recently in my Psychology of the African American Experience class, I lectured on academic disidentification. As I typically do when I give this lecture, I asked the students whether grades impact their self-esteem. To make the point even more salient, I told the students to think about a scenario where they receive a grade of "C" or lower on a test in their major. In a class that was about 60% Black, many of the students across racial and ethnic groups raised their hands. However, a disproportionately fewer number of African American students raised their hands.

Most noteworthy was the response of one of the African American male students, Devonte. Devonte was a senior and member of Omega Psi Phi Fraternity, Inc., a historically Black fraternity founded on the campus of Howard University. Devonte had the lowest grade in the class, in large part because he had three missing assignments. Devonte was clearly a bright student, as evidenced by his thoughtful (and often humorous) contributions to class discussions. He was obviously not the most conscientious student, as evidenced by his missing assignments and his sometimes late attendance to class. However, it was apparent that Devonte was popular among some of the Black students in the class. During the class discussion on academic disidentification, Devonte indicated that he did not base his self-esteem on his grades at all, and he talked about why he found that to be problematic. Devonte acknowledged that he had completely disidentified from school and that he was just trying to graduate. He was relatively dismissive of the worth and importance of grades, particularly in regard to his own definition of what it would mean to be successful. Prior to this lecture I have to confess that I found myself often frustrated with Devonte and questioning his motivation. It is indeed ironic that of all people, I would have such reactions to him.

After the academic disidentification lecture, I began to see Devonte in a different light. In many ways, he represents the prototypical bright, African American male student who has decided that he would not allow the domain of school to impact his self-worth. In his personal growth paper, Devonte made the following observation: "Honestly, I don't like school and I personally don't feel like it's for me ... Now don't get me wrong, there were a lot of things I could have done differently, a lot of books I could have read, and a lot of papers I could have done on time, but I have the tendency to occupy my time with work and organizational business and completely step around the work that needs to be done for school. I have this idea that when I forget an assignment I don't go to office hours, or email bomb my professor, I just stand on my manhood and take the failing grade. My GPA has steadily dropped since I arrived at the Forty Acres and on the outside I don't feel bad about it. But honestly I think about it and I realize that I have nothing to be happy about and the fact that my mother knows nothing about my grades lets me know that I am ashamed about it deep down inside. My GPA may be low but I'm not a dummy. I learned a lot in this class."

The process of academic disidentification is part of a more general set of processes referred to as psychological disengagement (Major & Schmader, 1998). Psychological disengagement refers to the disengagement of one's self-esteem from a particular domain. When the domain is academic, psychological disengagement is specifically referred to as academic disengagement or academic disidentification. Earlier I briefly reviewed the self-esteem literature and discussed the paradox of higher self-esteem among African American students in spite of having lower grades. While the paradoxical phenomenon has been identified in several studies reviewed, it is also important to better understand the reasons that might explain why the paradox exists. Two mechanisms have been proposed that account for the paradox: devaluing academic success and discounting academic feedback (Schmader, Major, & Gramzow, 2001).

DEVALUING ACADEMIC SUCCESS

Devaluing academic success involves attitudes that minimize the importance of making good grades and doing well in school. If African American students devalue academic success, making good grades will obviously not be important to them. In spite of the characterization of Black students as devaluing academic success, there is very little empirical evidence to support this assertion. Published studies that have explicitly and quantitatively examined devaluing academic success among African American students do not generally support this notion. As Schmader, Major, and Gramzow (2001) state, there is much evidence that demonstrates African American students value school at least as much as White students, and often times more.

In one study, Voelkl (1997) had a sample of 181 African American students and 1,150 White 8th-grade students taken from 104 schools. The students were part of a longitudinal study, and completed a 16-item measure of identification with school that reflected belongingness to school as well as valuing school and school-related outcomes. Voelkl found that African American students had higher levels of identification with school than White students. Grades were not related to identification with school among African American students, but they were related among White students.

In another study involving 676 undergraduate students at UCLA, differences among disengagement processes were examined (Schmader et al., 2001). There were 184 African American students, 270 Latino students, and 222 White students. Devaluing academic success was measured using four items: "Being good at academics is an important part of who I am," "Doing well on intellectual tasks is very important to me," "Academic success is not very valuable to me," and "It usually doesn't matter to me one way or the other how I do in school." The first two items were reverse scored. There were no ethnic group differences in devaluing academic success.

An important detail in these studies is how devaluing academic success is measured. Differences in wording or emphasis could produce discrepant results. On the other hand, if differences in wording or emphasis produce similar results, more definitive conclusions may be drawn. In a previously discussed study, Eccleston, Smyth, and Lopoo (2010) also examined differences in valuing academics between African American and White students. Valuing academic success was operationalized by two items that start off with the stem "for you being good in math is" and "for you being good in reading is." The response options ranged from 1 (not important) to 7 (very important). Two additional items addressed how useful math and reading were to them, with response options ranging from 1 (not at all useful) to 7 (very useful). Composite scores for valuing math and valuing reading were created. Eccleston et al. found that African American students were significantly higher in valuing both math and reading than White students. To further indirectly test the devaluing academics hypothesis, they examined whether math and reading self-concepts were predictive of self-esteem and found them both to be significantly predictive among African American and White students. The authors conclude that this data again do not support the hypothesis that African American students devalue academics.

Beyond examining mean group differences, it is also important to examine whether devaluing academic success is linked to GPA. The findings here are more equivocal. In one study with African American high school students, my colleagues and I found that devaluing academic success was not predictive of GPA (Cokley et al., 2011). However, in another study with African American college students, we found that devaluing academic success was predictive of GPA (Cokley & Chapman, 2008). However, when that data were disaggregated by gender, we found that devaluing academic success was correlated with GPA among African American females but not males (Cokley & Moore, 2007). It should be noted that the discrepancy in sample sizes (216 women, 58 men) may have contributed to the failure to find a significant relationship among men.

DISCOUNTING ACADEMIC FEEDBACK

Another reason that contributes to academic disidentification is the discounting of academic feedback. African American students often find it difficult to totally trust feedback or evaluations about their academic competencies when there is mistrust of the evaluation tool (e.g., standardized tests) or the evaluator (e.g., White teacher). The mistrust of White evaluators has long been established in the literature. Curtis Banks and his colleagues found that African American participants were less likely to engage in behavioral change when negative feedback came from White evaluators than when they came from Black evaluators (Banks, Stitt, Curtis, & McQuater, 1977). They also found that Black evaluators were perceived as more objective than White evaluators.

Given racial dynamics around cultural mistrust, what happens when a White evaluator gives critical feedback to Black and White students? Two experimental studies by Cohen, Steele, and Ross (1999) were conducted to answer this question. In the first study, students were asked to write a letter of commendation about their favorite teacher for possible publication in an education journal.

One week later, students received critical feedback about their letter, presumably from a White evaluator that pointed out weaknesses while also suggesting strategies for improvement. In one condition, students received only critical feedback (i.e., unbuffered criticism). In the second condition, students received the same critical feedback, coupled with an invocation of high standards along with the belief that the students could reach those standards (i.e., wise criticism). In the third condition, students received the same critical feedback, coupled with general praise of their performance (i.e., positive buffer). Students in all conditions were told that their photograph would be attached to their letters, which alerted the students that their racial identity would be known by the evaluator. When students received their letter and critical feedback a week later, it was signed by Gardiner Lindsay, which had been pretested as a recognizably White name. Black students in the unbuffered criticism condition rated the evaluator as more biased than White students. However, in the wise criticism condition, there was no race difference in rating the evaluator. Additionally, Black students in the unbuffered criticism condition rated the evaluator as more biased than Black students in the wise criticism condition. When the criticism was buffered by positive feedback, the ratings by Black and White students were smaller in difference in comparison to the unbuffered criticism condition, and there were virtually no differences in rating in the wise criticism condition.

In terms of motivation, Black students indicated lowered motivation in the unbuffered criticism condition compared to White students. In the wise criticism condition, Black students indicated somewhat higher motivation than White students. Similar to the ratings, the mean motivation for Black students in the positive criticism condition was in between the unbuffered and wise condition. The results of the second study were consistent with the first study and supported their hypotheses. The authors concluded that stigmatized students such as Black students will be concerned about whether they are being evaluated based on their merits or instead through the lens of a negative stereotype. This concern can present a challenge to the White evaluator or mentor in terms of effectively providing feedback to Black students without concerns of bias being raised. The authors conclude that wise criticism is better for Black students' self-efficacy than positive criticism or unbuffered criticism.

Recall that discounting academic feedback includes the mistrust of both the evaluator and the evaluation tool. There is additional support for racial/ethnic differences in discounting academic feedback. In the previously reviewed study, Schmader et al. (2001) found that African American students (and Latino American students) were more likely to discount test scores as biased than White students. Additional evidence of discounting academic feedback was found in the Eccleston et al. (2010) study, which found that the academic self-concept of African American students was less influenced by standardized test scores when compared to White students.

ACADEMIC MOTIVATION

The focus on stereotype threat, academic disidentification, devaluing academic success, and discounting academic feedback lead some observers to conclude that African American students have lower academic motivation than White students. Sandra Graham provides a comprehensive critique of the motivation literature regarding African Americans (Graham, 1994, 1997). She notes that the assumptions of African Americans as (1) lacking personality traits associated with achievement motivation, (2) being less likely to believe in internal or personal control of outcomes, and (3) having negative views of themselves because of lower academic achievement are not supported by empirical data.

Earlier, I discussed devaluing academic success and discounting academic feedback as mechanisms that allow African American students to maintain a high self-esteem in spite of lower academic performance. Another related mechanism is the attributions made by African American students to explain their lower academic performance. Van Laar (2000) conducted a longitudinal study where she found that African American students, like White students, were just as likely to make internal attributions about their success and failure as White students. In other words, when they do well or poorly African American students were just as likely to attribute their success or failure to ability and effort as White students. However, at the end of their first year, African American students began to make more external attributions about their failure than White students, and their expectations about future economic potential were lowered.

In an attempt to use diverse theoretical approaches to examine the academic motivation of African American students, I used self-determination theory given its popularity in the literature (Cokley, 2003). Self-determination theory proposes that human beings have three basic psychological needs of competence, autonomy, and relatedness that are essential for optimal functioning (Ryan & Deci, 2000). A basic assumption of self-determination theory is that all individuals have an innate need to be intrinsically motivated when their psychological needs are met.

Given the conventional wisdom that African American students have lowered academic motivation than White students, I conducted a study to test this assumption (Cokley, 2003). Using a sample of 394 African American students and 291 White students, I compared the motivation of both groups using the *Academic Motivation Scale* (Vallerand, Pelletier, Blais, & Brière, 1992). The *Academic Motivation Scale* measures both intrinsic and extrinsic motivation as well as amotivation (i.e., the lack of motivation). I found that African American and White students had similar levels of intrinsic motivation; however, African American students had significantly higher levels of all three types of extrinsic motivation than White students. Additionally, I found that the racial composition of the school environment was an important factor. African

American students attending historically Black colleges and universities (HBCUs) were significantly higher in all three types of intrinsic motivation than their counterparts at predominantly White colleges and universities (PWCUs). I concluded that (1) African American students do not lack academic motivation, (2) context matters, and (3) more research was needed to understand how African American students construct meaning around grades.

ANALYSIS AND CONCLUSIONS

As is the case in the previous chapters, this brief review of the literature examining the relationship between self-esteem and grades among African American students is not intended to be comprehensive in its coverage. There have been many empirical studies and scholarly treatments of academic disidentification, devaluing school, discounting academic feedback, and academic motivation (e.g., Graham, Taylor, & Hudley, 1998; Griffin, 2002; Morgan & Mehta, 2004; Tyson, 2002). The findings from these studies are generally consistent in their findings.

It was important to provide this brief review of empirical studies because of the general assumption that African American students do not value education and do not care about grades. By extension, an indictment is made about Black parents and their failure to cultivate the "proper" attitudes toward school. The sentiments are expressed seemingly innocently, such as when New York mayor Michael Bloomberg commented in the *New York Times* that there are some parents who have not had a formal education, and thus do not understand the value of an education. Some people interpreted his comments as essentially saying that Black parents have failed their kids because of not sufficiently valuing education. The attention and notoriety of people like John McWhorter, University of Texas at Austin law professor Lino Graglia, Republican state representative Jon Hubbard, and Bill Cosby (among many others including teachers and, unfortunately, some Black people themselves) fuel the belief that African Americans do not value education. In spite of this conventional wisdom, there is a profound misunderstanding and misinterpretation of Black students' self-esteem and self-concept around school and grades that has led to the mischaracterization of Blacks as not valuing education. This brief review of the literature therefore leads me to several conclusions.

First, in spite of the fact that African American students consistently are reported to have lower grades than White students, they maintain high levels of self-esteem and academic self-concept. To be clear, this does not mean that there is not the occasional Black student who does have lower self-esteem and/ or academic self-concept because of poor grades. These students certainly exist. However, study after study has consistently found that African American students, as a group, maintain relatively high self-esteem and academic self-concept even in the midst of lower academic achievement. Interventions designed to improve the academic achievement of African American students should probably not spend a lot of time focusing on raising their self-esteem or academic self-concept.

Related to this previous point, the process of academic disidentification among Black students is real. It is a well-documented phenomenon that is especially pronounced among Black males. Identification with school is important for all students in terms of positive academic outcomes, and students across race and ethnicity can experience some form of academic disidentification. However, it is clear that academic disidentification is more prevalent among Black students than other students. It is also clear that Black male students are the most likely of all student subgroups to become academically disengaged. Why Black male students are more prone to academic disidentification is not well understood. It has been suggested that the lack of Black male role models in the classroom has contributed to Black male motivation and disidentification with school (Cokley, 2001). As a result, Black males search for other Black male role models with whom they can identify and aspire to be like (e.g., athletes, rappers, etc.). This is consistent with social learning theory, which states that behavior is based on the process of observational learning (Bandura, 1977). Black males do not learn to identify with academics as fully as they might because they do not have the opportunity to learn this from other Black males. When I had my first Black male teacher in high school, a band teacher named Mr. Ferguson, I'll never forget the impact he had on my self-concept. However, the truth of the matter is that while psychologists and other social scientists have done a good job of documenting academic disidentification among Black males, as well as identifying the specific mechanisms of devaluing academic success and discounting academic feedback, it is not well understood how and why these mechanisms contribute to Black males being more prone to disidentification more than other groups.

The third conclusion that I draw is that there is very little empirical evidence that Black students devalue education and academic success more than White students. In fact, data often show that Black students actually value education and academic success more than White students. This conclusion may seem discrepant from the anecdotes people have, which would seem to support the characterization of Black students not valuing education. However, similar to the observations that I made about "acting White," I don't dispute that there are some Black students who may not value education. However, I do challenge the belief that the devaluing of education and academic success is unique and widespread among Black students. Of course, there are *some* Black students who devalue education and academic success, just as there are some White students, Asian students, Latino students, and Native students who may also devalue education and academic success. However, there is not a shred of empirical quantitative data that support the view that "most Blacks don't value education."

My fourth conclusion is that academic disidentification among Black students contributes to the myth of Black anti-intellectualism. When Black students maintain high self-esteem in spite of their grades, it may be interpreted as Black students simply not caring about school or education. However, there are several reasons, unrelated to anti-intellectualism, why the self-esteem of Black students is protected even in the face of lowered academic performance. Not linking grades to one's self-esteem cannot (or perhaps should not) be viewed as an example of Black anti-intellectualism. One can recognize and value the importance of going to school and getting an education without caring about grades because of concerns that grades can be biased and subjective.

My fifth conclusion is that there needs to be a much better understanding of the role of cultural mistrust in discounting academic feedback among Black college students. When the evaluators of Black students are White, it has been demonstrated that certain conditions must be met for Black students to trust the academic feedback they receive. When the evaluation tool is a standardized test, it is much more difficult to get Black students to trust the results. In fact, Cohen et al. (1999) found that the only way they could get Black students to trust the result of the test was to tell Black students that the creator of the test was also Black. Beyond that there was nothing they could say to make Black students trust the academic feedback from the standardized test. More interventions need to focus on how to increase the amount of trust that Black students have toward White evaluators.

In the final chapter, I reflect on the current state of Afrocentricity and briefly review the debate surrounding Afrocentric education. I discuss my experiences and successes using Afrocentric pedagogy to successfully engage African American students in the pursuit of self-knowledge. Through the use of videos, role playing, and an Afrocentric curriculum, I illustrate the importance of engaging the Black identity of African American students. I demonstrate that Black students are highly intrinsically motivated when they have a personal connection to the material they are being taught.

6

Afrocentric Pedagogy as a Tool for Motivating African American Students

> I was in pursuit of the definition of the role my own people had played in the
> history of the world; this had been my holy mission, my priesthood. You can-
> not successfully oppress a consciously historical people.
>
> —John Henrik Clarke

The 1980s and 1990s represented the zenith of the Afrocentric movement. Described as part of an ongoing "culture war" (Keita, 2000) at its best, Afrocentrism represented an educational challenge to the traditional Eurocentric canon of knowledge that marginalized the contributions of people of African descent. However, as is often the case with ideologies, the excesses of Afrocentrism generated intense and public scrutiny. There was perhaps no better illustration of this than the 1992 *New York Times* op-ed written by the African American intellectual and literary critic Henry Louis "Skip" Gates (Gates, 1992). In this op-ed Gates was responding to what he perceived as a disturbing trend in Black anti-Semitism. He linked the trend, in part, to a book that was popular among some people in the Afrocentric movement called *The Iceman Inheritance: Prehistoric Sources of Western Man's Racism, Sexism, and Aggression* (Bradley, 1991). The book controversially claims, among other things, that White people are essentially genetically predisposed to being racist, sexist, and aggressive because of being descended from Neanderthals. These notions have been coupled with presumed assumptions of White inferiority. This line of thinking has become a central tenet in certain expressions of Afrocentric thought, and has drawn the ire and rebuke of numerous African American scholars who believe, as Gates argued, that it represents Black demagoguery, pseudo scholarship, and an ill-fated attempt to raise the collective self-esteem of Black people. As I have previously reviewed, empirical data do not support the notion that Black people collectively suffer from low self-esteem. That said, there is a lingering belief that the attempts to infuse Afrocentric content and approaches to the educational curriculum for Black students is a sad, misguided attempt to make Black students feel better about themselves and their contributions to history.

In a much less heralded and publicized response to Gates's op-ed, the venerable Afrocentric scholar John Henrik Clarke published a response and dissenting view. He defended the Black scholars whom Gates criticized, and claimed that African people are "the most written about and the least understood people in the world." The motivation of Afrocentric scholars like John Henrik Clarke is in response to European scholars who, as stated by Clarke in his dissenting view, have basically implied or outright stated that Europeans brought light to a world waiting in darkness. Clarke discusses his own journey into becoming an Afrocentric scholar (though he does not use these exact words) in his book My *Life in Search of Africa* (Clarke, 1999). In the book Clarke recounts how his grandmother used to tell him stories about Africa, how he had a voracious appetite for reading history, and how he came to understand that Europeans colonized everything, from history to information about history, to the image of God as a White man. It was this sensibility that led Clarke to say in his dissenting view, "I could not find the image of my people in the Bible, so I began the search through the literature of the world until I found them and learned why some people considered it a necessity to leave African people out of the respectful commentary of history."

I start this final chapter with a reference to the old cultural wars related to Afrocentrism because I believe it is important to situate the criticisms of Afrocentrism within this historical context of perceived Black anti-intellectualism. Henry Louis Gates's characterization of certain proponents of Afrocentrism as Black demagogues and pseudo-scholars is another way of saying that Black folks, in this case Black professors, are anti-intellectual. In many ways, some may see a chapter on Afrocentric pedagogy to be anachronistic in 2014, especially given that the apex of debate about Afrocentricity occurred during the 1980s and 1990s. Nevertheless, I conclude with this chapter because of my successful experience with incorporating my own brand of Afrocentricity into the classroom over the past 16 years. There is a lingering sentiment, especially among academics with elite pedigrees, that Afrocentricity is a vulgar form of racial identity politics, not a viable intellectual paradigm, devoid of intellectual rigor and substance, and consequently not deserving of serious intellectual engagement. There is much evidence to support my belief that this is a lingering sentiment. For example, at highly ranked African American studies doctoral programs housed at prestigious universities such as Yale, Northwestern, UC-Berkeley, and Harvard, along with Michigan State and the University of Massachusetts at Amherst, there is little to no evidence of professors whose research and scholarly interests are related to Afrocentricity or any related variation (e.g., African-centered, Africentrism, Pan-Africanism). In my current departmental affiliation in African and African Diaspora Studies, aside from me that is certainly the case (with the possible exception of one or two individuals who quietly at least support in principle the idea of ideological diversity and intellectually engaging Afrocentricity). There seems to be an almost unspoken rule that certain intellectual discourses and paradigms are not welcome, indeed, are beneath the "high culture" and "high theory" focus of the Black intellectual elite who strive for academic respectability.

That is why I include this chapter on using Afrocentric pedagogy as a tool for motivating African American students. There is indeed a certain irony of using an ideological approach characterized as pseudo-scholarship and anti-intellectual to actually engage and motivate Black students to care about school and to excel academically. In this chapter I briefly review how Afrocentric principles have been researched and applied in educational contexts among Black students. Additionally, I reflect on my experiences using Afrocentric pedagogy to successfully engage African American students in the passionate pursuit of self-knowledge. Specifically, I discuss the success of my Psychology of the African American Experience class, which students frequently describe as a life-altering experience. Through the use of videos, role playing, and an Afrocentric curriculum, students experience a sense of excitement and passion for learning that has often been missing from much of their education. I illustrate the importance of engaging the Black identity of African American students, and demonstrate that they are highly intrinsically motivated when they have a personal connection to the material they are being taught. Using excerpts from personal growth papers, I provide evidence of the pedagogical effectiveness and impact of a class that is explicitly Afrocentric in focus and practice.

BLACK CULTURAL LEARNING STYLES: FACT OR FICTION?

As previously mentioned, the 1980s and 1990s were the zenith of the Afrocentric movement. In educational circles, the idea of Black cultural learning styles was a popular idea that represented one manifestation of the influence of Afrocentric ideology. The idea of Black cultural learning styles was popularized by the early childhood educator Janice Hale-Benson in her book *Black Children: Their Roots, Culture, and Learning Styles* (Hale-Benson, 1986). Additionally, Madge Willis, a school psychologist, provided a review of the literature on learning styles of African American children (Willis, 1989). Hale-Benson and Willis, both African American, argued for the existence of Black cultural learning styles, which, if understood and incorporated into pedagogy, could improve the academic outcomes of African American students. Various Black psychologists had provided conceptual writings detailing how African American culture was different and distinct from White culture (Boykin & Toms, 1985; Hilliard, 1976; McAdoo & McAdoo, 1985; Nobles, 1974). Hilliard (1976, p. 41) provided a taxonomy of school learning styles of (a) school as it is in general, and (b) school as it could be, that roughly corresponded with the cultural learning styles of White and Black students, respectively. An abbreviated version is presented in Table 6.1.

The idea of a cultural mismatch in learning styles became a popular explanation for Black student underachievement. Such ideas contributed to the creation

Table 6.1
The Learning Style of the School

School as It Is in General	School as It Could Be
Rules	Freedom
Standardization	Variation
Conformity	Creativity
Regularity	Novelty
Memory for specific facts	Memory for essence
Egocentric	Sociocentric
Controlled	Expressive
Universal Meanings	Contextual Meanings
Cognitive	Affective
Isolation	Integration
Object-focused	People-focused

Note: Abbreviated excerpt from *Alternatives to IQ testing: An approach to the identification of gifted minority children (final report)* by Asa G. Hilliard, 1976 (p. 41). San Francisco, CA: California State Department of Education, Special Education Support Unit.

of Afrocentric schools and schools catered to young Black males. One of the more controversial responses was the creation of a pamphlet that was published by the New York State Board of Regents to address the high dropout rate of ethnic minority students. According to a *New York Times* article, the pamphlet promoted the idea of Black students having a learning style not supported by schools as being a contributing factor to the high dropout rate (DePalma, 1990). In her review of the literature, Willis (1989) makes the following observation: "Cooperation is an important dimension in African American children's learning style" (p. 53). She cites the research of Slavin and Oickle (1981), who found that cooperative learning groups, which include small, heterogeneous ability groups working together on learning tasks and activities, are especially effective for Black students.

Proponents of Black cultural learning styles generated a lot of attention and, predictably, criticisms. One notable criticism was by Craig Frisby, an African American school psychology professor. Frisby wrote a fairly scathing article in which he argued that there were serious flaws with the five major assumptions of Black cultural learning styles (Frisby, 1993). He identified those major assumptions as follows:

1. Within America, Black and White culture is fundamentally incompatible
2. Characteristics of Black culture "determine" the learning style of Black children

3. Learning style assessment is reliable and valid
4. Black learners are incapable of manifesting any behavior that is different from behaviors dictated by their identified cultural learning style; therefore, teachers are morally obligated to adapt their instructional practices to Black children's identified learning styles
5. There are "culture-specific" educational prescriptions that are uniquely effective in increasing academic achievement for Black students relative to Whites

Frisby then methodically examines each of these assumptions and attempts to debunk them through a combination of logic and research. One of his central and notable questions is whether methods attributed to Afrocentric interventions (e.g., including high levels of motor activity and stimulation; teachers exhibiting warmth; incorporating intense, group-oriented, interpersonal learning experiences rather than individual seatwork; and incorporating role-playing and sociodramatic teaching strategies) were really new and uniquely effective for Black children. He argued that these methods are not new, and in fact, no different from models found in early childhood education. More importantly, he argued that there was no empirical research to support many of these so-called Afrocentric interventions. Citing the research of Thomas Sowell (1986) on six academically successful predominantly Black public and private schools, he highlighted the following findings:

1. Race of the principal was unrelated to school success
2. Background characteristics of students were similar in successful and failing schools
3. The presence or absence of Black history was largely irrelevant to the success of schools
4. Student individual differences of ability vary between schools
5. Discipline characterized by a "law and order" philosophy was a prominent characteristic

Frisby concluded by saying that the reasons for continued support of Black cultural learning styles was because of conclusions drawn from (1) flawed research, (2) pseudoscientific theories of African American culture, (3) fear of being labeled insensitive or racially disloyal because of critiquing Black cultural learning styles, (4) hypersensitivity to any explanation perceived as a deficit model, and (5) failure of current educational practices to successfully educate African American children. Frisby warns us that the Black cultural learning styles theory (i.e., Afrocentric approach) is eerily reminiscent of nineteenth-century racist educational philosophy. He concludes that more focus should be placed on individual differences rather than group stereotypes. Not surprisingly, Frisby's article generated thoughtful, but critical responses (Hale, 1993; Richardson, 1993). Hale argued that Frisby misrepresented the suggestions made by Afrocentric scholars, and that he offered no solutions for how to improve the educational outcomes for Black children. Richardson takes Frisby to task for overlooking the role of historical experiences as well as for holding little regard for Black culture.

The debates about Black cultural learning styles, similar to and perhaps in concert with Afrocentrism, reached their peak during the 1990s. An examination of the literature reveals that very little additional work has been conducted on this topic. It is tempting to conclude that the topic is passé and of little theoretical and practical significance today. However, I believe that would be a misreading and misunderstanding of the literature. While the term Black cultural learning style does not appear to be in vogue today, there is still attention being given to the idea that culture plays an important role in the achievement of Black students. In my opinion, no researcher has been more effective in identifying the role of culture in Black students' achievement than Wade Boykin.

AFRO-CULTURAL VALUES: COMMUNALISM, MOVEMENT, AND VERVE

Wade Boykin was trained as an experimental social psychologist at the University of Michigan. Currently the codirector of the National Center for Research on the Education of Students as well as professor of psychology at Howard University, he has conducted an impressive program of research examining cultural influences of Black students' achievement. While a comprehensive review of his studies is warranted to fully appreciate the significance of his work, I will provide a cursory review of his theoretical work and then briefly review a handful of his studies to highlight some of their important findings.

At the core of Boykin's work is the idea that the cultural environment plays an important role in the achievement of African American students. He identifies three Afro-cultural themes that are prevalent in African American culture and thus have educational implications (Boykin, 1986). The themes are communalism, movement, and verve. Communalism refers to the importance placed on social bonds and interconnectedness with others. Movement refers to the importance placed on expressiveness, dance, rhythm, and music. Verve refers to the preference for heightened levels of physical stimulation. Boykin theorizes that these three themes are commonly found in the homes and environments of African Americans.

Boykin and his collaborators have conducted a number of studies examining these Afrocultural themes. In one study, Marryshow, Hurley, Allen, Tyler, and Boykin (2005) examined the perceptions of 90 African American children toward four high achievers who employed different orientations toward schooling and achievement. Two of the high achievers were characterized as individualistic or competitive (representing mainstream values), while the other two high achievers were characterized as preferring communalism and verve (representing African American cultural variables). Students also reported their perceptions of what types of high achievers teachers would prefer. Results indicated that students rated the verve and communal high achievers significantly higher than the individualistic or competitive high achievers. Students also believed that teachers would have more favorable attitudes toward high achievers who were individualistic and competitive. The authors conclude that African American students do value academic achievement when it can be achieved in a mode that is culturally familiar to them.

In an extension of the previous study Tyler, Boykin, Miller, and Hurley (2006) examined 80 African American children's perceptions toward four high achievers, as well as their perceptions of what their parents and peers would prefer. Similar to the previous study, results indicated that students rated the verve and communal high achievers significantly higher than the individualistic or competitive high achievers. Additionally, students' perceptions of what their parents and peers would prefer yielded similar findings. The authors conclude that students have a clear preference for high-achieving students who have African American cultural values.

While I am a proponent of conducting research only using African Americans as a way to better understand behavior in indigenous cultural terms (what has been referred to as an emic approach), I also recognize that comparative research involving White students can, under certain conditions, offer important insights. One study that accomplished this was conducted by Ellison, Boykin, Tyler, and Dillihunt (2005). In this study, 66 African American and 72 White fifth- and sixth-grade students in a low income community completed measures of three learning preferences: cooperative, competitive, and individualistic. Results indicated that there was a preference for cooperative learning over competitive and individualistic learning among both African American and White students. However, African American students reported significantly higher preferences for cooperative learning than White students, while White students reported significantly higher preferences for competitive and individualistic learning. The authors conclude that teachers should accept, incorporate, and recognize culturally diverse learning preferences.

Most of the studies examining learning preferences focus on middle school students. I am unaware of any published studies of this nature that have been conducted among college students. However, a colleague and I published a study comparing dimensions of individualism and collectivism among African American and White students (Komarraju & Cokley, 2008). We found that African American students were higher on horizontal individualism (i.e., preference for uniqueness and freedom to express themselves) than White students, while White students were higher on vertical individualism (i.e., preference to be independent and competitive). One unexpected finding was the correlation between individualism, collectivism, and GPA. There was a significant positive correlation between collectivism and GPA among African American students but not White students. These findings are consistent with Boykin's research showing that African American students prefer learning that emphasizes communalism rather than individualism.

AFRICAN-CENTERED EDUCATION

For some individuals, the chronic underachievement of African American students is attributed to what is perceived to be a cultural mismatch in terms of values, content, and pedagogy. One response has been the creation of African-centered schools, which share one basic assumption: that every child can achieve success. Children are not seen as "at-risk" or "disadvantaged"; rather, they are seen as having unlimited potential that needs to be tapped into by teachers. African-centered schools, like single-sex schools, have generated controversy because of the notion that African American students cannot excel academically in traditional, mainstream educational settings. Critics have suggested that it is insulting to assume that African American students are fundamentally different and need a different educational process to achieve. Other critics have suggested that it is too narrowly focused on one racial group. Some have even implied that it is dangerously close to being driven by racist assumptions about Blacks (Frisby, 1993). In some instances these concerns seem to be well intentioned (even if misguided), while in other instances they seem to be duplicitous. In either case, there appears to be failure to objectively examine African-centered schools to determine if they are making a positive impact. In this regard, several African-centered schools should be acknowledged.

One such school is the Marcus Garvey School, which was created in 1975 by Dr. Anyim Palmer. Located in Los Angeles, California, the Marcus Garvey School is a nonprofit, private school with an Afrocentric curriculum. The school has gained notoriety because of third and fourth graders doing algebra and fifth graders doing trigonometry and calculus, as well as sending seventh graders to various colleges. The teachers believe that students should not be taught with a "one size fits all" approach. In addition to having daily exposure to the five core subjects of math, English, spelling, reading, and penmanship, students are taught science, the importance of good health, Swahili, Spanish, world geography, African history, U.S. history, world history, and computer technology. Given the importance of math, students are taught at math levels that are two to five grade levels above state standard mandates.

In the April 27, 1998, *U.S. News & World Report*, the African-centered school Sankofa Shule was described as an "educational powerhouse of charter schools." Located in Lansing, Michigan, and opening in 1995, Sankofa was one of the first charter schools in Lansing. The school is described as combining African and African American history with a Montessori-styled curriculum. Sankofa's educational success was lauded by several media outlets, including the

Wall Street Journal and *U.S. News & World Report,* and became a model for other African-centered schools. According to Shariba Rivers, daughter of the founder Dr. Freya Rivers, Sankofa's guiding principles included ancient Kemetic/Egyptian principles of Maat and Ptah Hotep, along with the principles of Dr. Maulana Karenga's Nguzo Saba from his Kawaida theory (Rivers, 2010). The curriculum included the standard curriculum of science, language arts, mathematics, history, French, and Spanish, along with less common curriculum such as Swahili, martial arts, African dance, and African drumming. Policy and practice in areas such as discipline were guided by African-centered principles and concerns for the student's physical, emotional, and spiritual health. For example, children were not suspended from school because of bad behavior; instead, parents left work to attend school and work with the teachers and their children. Dr. Rivers also did not think that certification through traditional teacher education programs was the best way to ensure teacher competence for African American students. Instead, teachers were in a constant state of self-actualization through serious discussions every morning. These meetings typically involved (1) reading from a cultural and educational text, (2) conversations about students that focused on their overall well-being, and (3) discussing successful teaching strategies based on classroom observations.

In the June 8, 2006, edition of the *Christian Science Monitor,* an article was written about J. S. Chick Elementary School, a public magnet school in Kansas City, Missouri, that was transformed into an African-centered school in 1991. In a school where 99% of its 300 students were African American, Chick was recognized for having test scores that exceeded the state average. Chick was described as having a curriculum based on the history and culture of the African diaspora. Having high test scores was only one way the school was seen as being successful. Success was also measured by the fact that students learn to see themselves as leaders and contributors to the community. Chick empowers students by incorporating African cultural traditions and helping students to see their place within the world of learning. Teachers, parents, and students are greeted with *Jambo,* a Swahili word meaning hello. Drumming, dancing, and self-affirming chants are part of the culture of Chick. While there has not been a rigorous experimental study to determine any causal links to achievement connected with Chick's curriculum and approach, one often-reported statistic was that 48% of Chick students were deemed to be proficient or advanced on the Missouri Assessment Program, compared to the statewide averages of 24% for Black students and 36% for White students.

IMPACT OF PSYCHOLOGY OF THE AFRICAN AMERICAN EXPERIENCE CLASS

In the Introduction for this book, I briefly mentioned the impact that the class Psychology of the African American Experience had on Black college students.

I said that teaching this class has been without a doubt the most fulfilling aspect of being a professor. I mentioned that teaching this class has allowed me to see a level of enthusiasm, motivation, and achievement from African American students that energizes me and serves as a reminder about why I became a professor. I also mentioned that I have made this same observation at every institution where I have been privileged to teach. Teaching this class has proven to be a powerful and transformative experience, and has demonstrated to me that the notion that African American students have problems with academic motivation is indeed a myth. The class is explicitly Afrocentric in its orientation. I can think of no better way to illustrate the impact of the class and to demonstrate the efficacy of utilizing an Afrocentric approach than sharing the words of the students themselves. I have selected a few of the many quotes that I have read from personal growth papers over the years. I believe these quotes convey the impact this class has had on their lives. Some students compared this class to other "traditional" psychology classes.

> As a psychology major at UT, I know first hand the one sidedness of the entire psychology department. Even though I love my major, I have found the excitement that I had once before to be diminishing over time. Practically all of the research articles and studies I have read have nothing to do with me, so it becomes quite difficult for me to remain interested. If a study of African Americans is brought up, it is never discussed in much detail. . . . I also appreciated how Dr. Cokley didn't just let these discussions go off on a tangent about nothing. We discussed facts and research. By the end of the course I noticed another change in myself. When Dr. Cokley did present certain statistics from research, I questioned them more. I wanted to know about the sampling, the circumstances of the participants, and the overall validity of the study in reference to African Americans. I was thinking even more like someone of my future profession.
>
> It was during my freshman year of college that I decided to become exposed to the subject and take an intro psych course. In this class I learned about many controversial psychologists such as Freud, Pavlov, and Skinner, and their experiments (i.e., Pavlov's Dogs, Milgram Shock Experiment, and the Bystander Experiment). While being a member of this class a few things bothered me: (1) There were no African Americans in this class, (2) I didn't hear anything about any famous black psychologists, and (3) None of these teachings resonated with me as a black man . . . In this class, [Psychology of African American Experience] it made me happy to be provided a racial view of a very interesting subject for a change.
>
> As a psychology major, I have learned to do something in this course which has not been emphasized in my previous psychology courses which was to think of the African and African American experience from a psychological perspective. I anticipated taking this course having heard personal testimonies from my African American peers who described it as life-changing, original, and the truth.

Other students talked about how the class has changed their thoughts, attitudes, and behavior.

This course has caused me to revamp my whole thought process in terms of the importance of education, the realness of racism, the history and psychological impact of oppression, power via hegemony. . . . Now I feel less gullible, am more skeptical of previous lessons about my ancestors taught in grade school.

One of the things that really change the way I thought about my own beliefs was the classroom discussion that surrounded the "N" word and Dr. Cokley's own personal views on it. The word is [the] subject of much controversy in the black community. The historical roots of this word ties it to oppression and racism and for many blacks it will never be an acceptable word, but for some it has been adopted as a term of endearment amongst each other. Dr. Cokley's opinion about it made me realize the seriousness of the word and no matter how we try to dress it up, it is still a word that has caused our ancestors anguish. That class discussion really opened my eyes to what I was saying, and how much me saying that word contradicts everything I stand for.

And though the vast majority of the courses I have taken at UT during my first year have been extremely informative and interesting, none of them seem to compare to the magnitude of which Dr. Cokley's Psychology of the African American Experience class has affected my perception of the world and my personal life . . . I honestly believe this course has also allowed me to grow and change in ways that have really helped me to deal with certain personal issues related to my experience as an African American student.

Some students talked about how the class motivated them to engage in further discussions outside class and to continue learning by conducting further research.

This information I learn in this course definitely goes outside of the classroom with me. I have discussion with my roommates or friends about topics that caused so much debate during our classes. When I tell people everything that we discussed in class for that day their first reactions are always "I want to take that class." This class has also helped me to stop using the phrase "acting white" to describe an African American person who does not live up to my standards of what I think "acting black" is.

In all honesty I learned too much and too little in this class which turns out to be the perfect mix of emotions I need to continue studying African American people and culture . . . Though I came into the class with an interest in studying minorities in the media, the topics we discussed only intensified my yearning to know more. I have found myself searching for more literature that covers the same subjects in order to gain an even deeper understanding of the history and affects [sic] of racism on the African American experience . . . After almost every discussion that we had in class, I have gone off and talked to my peers about the subject as if I had to implant/warn the masses about the issues that are affecting our society.

As a result of being exposed to different scholars I have began [sic] to do my own research, I realized that I was always interested in African American culture, but I always read from one perspective and the different scholars excited me in a different way.

Interestingly, and contrary to negative characterizations of Afrocentric approaches as being too narrow and ethnocentric, some students made comments about becoming more open-minded.

> Having a new understanding of societal hurdles being a universal issue, I now understand that there is no one, singular, authentic "Black Experience," because no one person has the same life or deals with the same problems. With this new outlook I now embrace my black peers from all walks of life, and value their opinions, stories, and wisdom because they offer a window of understanding that I could not open by myself. This class has taken me out of my comfort zone and in turn has been the catalyst for me becoming a more open enlightened and understanding individual.
>
> This class has definitely made me see a lot of things differently! How I see myself, the world, my community, the media, other cultures, etc. has changed and I'm more open-minded and conscious about things.
>
> More than anything this class has taught me to be a more open-minded person.

Some students talked about having a new or renewed commitment to serving the Black community.

> This class has opened my eyes even more to see the problems that the African American culture faces each and every day. It has motivated me to be more active in the African American community by fighting for justice and advocating for change. I plan to get into the community and begin to change things for the betterment of African Americans.
>
> As a result of miseducation of the community, I have decided that I would work with different school districts to promote classes that teach students about African American history from beginning to end.

Consistent with the research of Dr. Wade Boykin, some students mentioned cultural themes that resonated with them.

> Coming from a predominantly black school, this class made me feel like I was at home. Each day, my soul could not wait till the clock struck 12:15, that's the time I would be leaving my ASL class and heading to EDP class. The class was such a soulful class, it became my most favorite class out of the years I've been here at UT.
>
> [M]y life has been enriched through the intellectual and social connection I have made with other students in the class. And such connections would not have been possible if it were not for Dr. Cokley's structuring of the class, which allows for tons of discourse, debate, and critical thinking and analysis. Furthermore, Dr. Cokley himself has been a great professor. He does not seem to try to make students think or feel a certain way, he tries to get his students to think critically. And his easy-going and laid back attitude definitely makes the class have a more communal feel. A truly unforgettable class!
>
> You portrayed an African-American who is capable of uniting a group of peers into one big family (collectivism). This is one of the few courses where I can

honestly say I felt an equal amount of respect between all peers—not once did I feel that one of us was at a disadvantage.

Not surprisingly, many comments from students reflected their increased Black consciousness.

Because I have reconstructed my definition of Blackness, I no longer strive to succeed in spite of being Black, but instead, acknowledge my Blackness as aiding me in my success and understanding of the world. I not only understand, but I can identify with other African Americans who recognize the impact their race plays on their lives. Black is hardworking; Black is the way we talk and the music we listen to; Black is our kinky hair; Black is acknowledging and appreciating the plight of our ancestors, and Black is resilient and to be celebrated.

When a Black child grows up and reads history books and sees that other ethnic groups have histories painted with glory and discovery how do they feel about their own ancestors? Their history is painted as one of bondage and servitude. . . . I think the first thing that needs to be done deals with the type of language we use . . . I remember recounting the story of my friends and I and the hand games we used to play. "Step back Jack, your hands too black. You lookin' like a monkey on a railroad track." As a seven year old girl I didn't understand how what I was saying could be harmful or hurtful but when I recited these same words to a male peer, it was evident. If I hear some of the little girls saying this, I plan to nip it in the bud right there and explain to them in the best of my abilities why this is wrong.

This class has also helped change the way I look at myself as a Black woman. I used to try to separate myself from the Black community because of the social schemas and negative stereotypes often associated with Black people and, more specifically Black women . . . For a long while, I allowed such mental slavery to keep me from connecting with those whose identities intersect with mine. However, in taking Psychology of the African American Experience along with Critical Perspectives in Black Women's Writing, I am growing to embrace a new level of self-identification and agency.

This particular AFR class . . . has been the most thought-provoking, insightful, and sometimes emotionally draining (in a necessary sense) three hours of my weekly life. . . . It donned [sic] on me that there is a significant amount of cognitive dissonance that is created when an individual seeks black pride, but has nothing but the genocide that is known as American slavery to reference to as a source of history.

All the information from the videos was new and exciting. Honestly, sometimes I feel intimidated by being the only black person in my classes. Because I am one of maybe seven black people in my entire major of nursing I feel discouraged . . . but those days are gone. To hear that your people, black people were the actual first people, has stuck with me ever since. When I think of Egypt and Egyptian people, I now think of black people. I think of an African Eve who we all came from and feel motivated. Now when I sit in my classes and ever feel alone, I remind myself that black people had the first working civilizations and have contributed much to this world. If I ever start to doubt my worth, my contribution, or my intelligence,

I remember these videos and my real black history, which debunks my insecurities ... This class has impacted my self-esteem and self-worth.

Bottom line was I did not want to be called dark because, dark people aren't pretty, or intelligent. I thought I was both of those things which were the main reasons that I did not want to be considered dark. When Dr. Cokley asked the class why "African Booty Scratcher" was funny I had to question my own sense of humor. I always thought I was pro black but I still found hurtful terminology funny. I dug deep into my own conscious [sic] and I found that the term was funny because I had disassociated myself from being African, to me I was simply Black, which boiled down to Non African. After coming to the realization that I was African, I understood that I was not the only black person with the misinterpretation that I wasn't African.

ANALYSIS AND CONCLUSIONS

As I have said about the previous chapters, this chapter was not intended to be a comprehensive review of the literature on the impact of Afrocentric pedagogy. There are much more extensive treatments of Afrocentric pedagogy and education to which readers should be directed. For example, Diane Pollard and Cheryl Ajirotutu (2000) have edited a book that tells the story of an African-centered elementary and middle school. The premise of the book is that schools that are immersed in African traditions, symbols, and values are more congruent with the values, lifestyles, and cultures of African American families. Peter Murrell (2002) has written a book on African-centered pedagogy, where he argues that current ineffective educational frameworks can be made more effective if reinterpreted through an African-centered lens. Kmt Shockley has also written articles on Afrocentric education (Shockley, 2007; Shockley & Frederick, 2010) and being an Afrocentric teacher (Shockley, 2011).

I have suggested that the Afrocentric movement reached its zenith during the 1980s and 1990s during a period rife with debates related to "cultural wars." Some have argued that Afrocentrism is a "dying pseudohistory," and that it was a race-centric approach to history that, while understandable given academic racism, is nevertheless an intellectually specious and inadequate response to Black students' academic underachievement. Interestingly, educators, psychologists, and social workers have been more open to Afrocentrism than other disciplines by applying Afrocentric principles in the classroom and to mental health practices. While concerned about theory, the disciplines of education, psychology, and social work ultimately are especially concerned about how the practical application of Afrocentric principles can produce positive educational and mental health outcomes for Black students. This brief review of the literature and my 16 years of teaching Psychology of the African American Experience from an Afrocentric perspective lead me to draw several conclusions.

First, there are different expressions of Afrocentrism that vary considerably in terms of historical claims and attitudes toward White people. Some proponents of Afrocentrism have been characterized as "vulgar nationalists" whose "reactionary racism . . . is beyond the reach of normal discourse" (Cross, 1991, p. 213). This expression of Afrocentrism is perceived as making outlandish and unsubstantiated historical claims of ancient African greatness (e.g., Black Africans were the creators of civilization; Cleopatra was a Black African queen; Beethoven was Black; ancient Egyptians were Black; Greeks and Romans stole African culture; Black Africans invented philosophy, medicine, writing, technology, science, etc.) to which contemporary African Americans can lay claim. Additionally, this expression of Afrocentrism is often coupled with anti-White attitudes (e.g., biological inferiority of Whites because of the lack of melanin; hatred of Whites) which sometimes manifests in anti-Jewish attitudes (e.g., Jews being primarily responsible for the Atlantic slave trade). It is important to recognize that, as is the case with other intellectual paradigms, scholars can reasonably disagree on certain issues. For example, as much as some White and Black scholars have dismissed the notion that ancient Egyptians were Black, there is ample evidence to indicate that they were most assuredly not White and that we could consider them today to be "people of color." Surely this is worth Black students (really, all students) being exposed to and debating among themselves. While I personally believe that ancient Egyptians were what we consider in modern terms to be "Black" and/or "African," I am also comfortable with their being recognized as people of color, as long as they are not referred to as European or White. Additionally, I believe the expression of Afrocentrism that is vehemently anti-White is not productive or healthy for Black students. Afrocentricity does not, as Asante (1991) states, "convert you by appealing to hatred or lust or greed or violence" (p. 6). There is a difference in cultivating an awareness of racism and White supremacy (which I think is totally appropriate and necessary for Black survival) versus cultivating an extreme dislike bordering on abject hatred of White people and White culture. Afrocentricity should do the former and avoid the latter. My previous research has shown that even the word Afrocentric is misunderstood or narrowly defined (Cokley, 2002). For example, in one study, I found that in response to the question "What does it mean to be Afrocentric?" 24% of the responses of African American students linked Afrocentricity to anti-Whiteness or an extreme form of ethnocentrism (Cokley, 2005). Afrocentricity, as I understand and practice it, is a "radical critique of the Eurocentric ideology" (Asante, 1998, p. 1) that ultimately is "not hegemonic" and is "essential to human harmony" (Asante, 1999).

Second, there is reasonable empirical evidence to indicate that Black students tend to prefer certain cultural learning environments over others. This is not to say that all Black students in all circumstances prefer the exact same cultural learning environment. One would be incredibly naïve to suggest this. For example, contrary to prevailing conventional wisdom, empirical research has not shown Black people to be lower in individualism than White people. In fact, meta-analyses have actually shown Black people to exhibit among the highest levels of individualism in comparison to Whites, Asians, and Latinos (Coon & Kemmelmeier, 2001; Oyserman, Coon, & Kemmelmeier, 2002). On the other hand, what makes the psychology of African Americans (and therefore Black students) more complicated is the fact that research also suggests that African Americans are also higher in collectivism than White people (Coon & Kemmelmeier, 2001; Gaines, Larbie, Patel, Pereira, & Sereke-Melake, 2005) while other scholars suggest that there are no differences (Oyserman et al., 2002). Nevertheless, the work of Wade Boykin and his colleagues is building a strong case for the premise that Black students tend to prefer certain learning environments that emphasize the Afrocultural themes of communalism, movement, and verve. In addition to the growing empirical evidence, I have years of anecdotal evidence teaching the Psychology of the African American Experience class that support this premise. My use of humor, role plays, encouraging lively debate, taking the occasional opportunity to take pop quizzes in small groups and to use a "lifeline" with other students for help, and having the class final in groups of 5–7 students have all resonated very positively with my Black students. Classes with predominantly Black students invariably take on a certain ethos and character, and fostering an Afrocultural learning environment seems to be the most conducive and effective way of fully engaging them and maximizing their learning.

Third, Afrocentric pedagogy is not the only way to engage Black students and improve their achievement. There is truth in the idea that certain educational and pedagogical principles will be effective with Black students in spite of the fact that they are not explicitly rooted in Afrocentrism. For example, the importance of student-teacher relationships is central in Black student achievement. Teachers must show that they genuinely care about students. Additionally, teachers must have high expectations for Black students. Lowering expectations for Black students out of some paternalistic notion about perceptions of their ability and intelligence does not help them, and in many ways does them much more harm than good. Caring for Black students and having consistently high expectations for them are not exclusively "Afrocentric" principles. They are simply sound educational and pedagogical principles. If there is an advantage of using an Afrocentric pedagogy, it is related to the "type" of Black student and citizen that is being produced. I agree with Mwalimu Shujaa that Afrocentric education helps Black people to determine what is in our interests, to distinguish our interests from the interests of other people, and to recognize the consistency and inconsistency of those interests (Shujaa, 2003). In short, while Afrocentric pedagogy cannot take credit as being the only means through which to improve

African American student achievement, it can take credit for instilling a type of Black consciousness that will likely lead to producing a more civically engaged citizen who is invested in improving the conditions of the Black community.

Finally, I end with the reason why I wrote this book, which was to challenge the idea that Black students are anti-intellectual. My goal was to write this book to make the best of psychological and educational research accessible to the masses, and to specifically show that this research paints a very different picture of Black students than conventional wisdom. I have used anecdotes from my own personal history along with references to popular culture and social science research to make the case that Black students are not anti-intellectual. I have made the argument that Black students are actually very intellectual and inquisitive and engaged, particularly when they see themselves reflected in the curriculum and when they are taught by culturally competent teachers. The excerpts from the personal growth papers show examples of students who are highly motivated, engaged, and transformed from being in a class that was rooted in their experiences. Certainly, all classes cannot be taught that way, because all classes are not about the Black experience. However, classes can be taught in a way that the lived experiences and history of Black people are made to be salient in some meaningful manner. Black students want to feel that they (in the truly corporate sense of their race/ethnicity/culture) matter and have contributed to the course of human civilization. Black students are generally concerned about their communities, and they want to contribute to improving the material conditions of their communities. Their hope is that education is the vehicle through which this can happen. When education does not address this most basic of psychological needs, it may understandably be seen as irrelevant. Black students should not be viewed as anti-intellectual because of what is essentially the failure of their education to be relevant to their lives as Black people.

Bibliography

Ainsworth-Darnell, J. W., & Downey, D. B. (1998). Assessing the oppositional culture explanation for racial/ethnic differences in school performance. *American Sociological Review, 63*, 536–553.

Akbar, N. (1996). *Breaking the chains of psychological slavery.* Tallahassee, FL: Mind Productions & Associates.

Akbar, N. (1998). *Know thy self.* Tallahassee, FL: Mind Productions & Associates.

Alexander, M. (2012). *The new Jim Crow: Mass incarceration in the age of colorblindness.* New York, NY: New Press.

Allen, B. A., & Boykin, A. W. (1992). African American children and the educational process: Alleviating cultural discontinuity through prescriptive pedagogy. *School Psychology Review, 21*(4), 586–596.

Altschul, I., Oyserman, D., & Bybee, D. (2006). Racial-ethnic identity in mid-adolescence: Content and change as predictors of academic achievement. *Child Development, 77*(5), 1155–1169.

American Psychiatric Association (Ed.). (2000). *Diagnostic and statistical manual of mental disorders: DSM-IV-TR.* Washington, DC: American Psychiatric Publishing.

Asante, M. K. (1980). *Afrocentricity: The theory of social change.* Trenton, NJ: African World Press.

Asante, M. K. (1990). *Kemet, Afrocentricity, and knowledge.* Trenton, NJ: Africa World Press.

Asante, M. K. (1991). *Afrocentricity.* Trenton, NJ: Africa World Press.

Asante, M. K. (1998). *The Afrocentric idea.* Philadelphia, PA: Temple University Press.

Asante, M. K. (1999). *The painful demise of Eurocentrism.* Trenton, NJ: Africa World Press.

Asante, M. K. (2006). A discourse on Black studies: Liberating the study of African people in the Western academy. *Journal of Black Studies, 36*(5), 646–662.

Awad, G. (2007). The role of racial identity, academic self-concept, and self-esteem in the prediction of academic outcomes for African American students. *Journal of Black Psychology, 33*, 188–207.

Azibo, D. (1992). Articulating the distinction between Black studies and the study of Blacks: The fundamental role of culture and the African-centered worldview. *The Afrocentric Scholar: The Journal of the National Council for Black Studies, 1*(1), 64–97.

Bahr, M. W., Fuchs, D., Stecker, P. M., & Fuchs, L. S. (1991). Are teachers' perceptions of difficult-to-teach students racially biased? *School Psychology Review, 20*(4), 599–608.

Bailey, C. T., & Boykin, A. W. (2001). The role of task variability and home contextual factors in the academic performance and task motivation of African American elementary school children. *Journal of Negro Education, 70*(1–2), 84–95.

Baldwin, J. A. (1979). Theory and research concerning the notion of Black self-hatred: A review and reinterpretation. *Journal of Black Psychology, 5*(2), 51–77. doi:10.1177/009579847900500201

Bandura, A. (1977). *Social learning theory.* Englewood Cliffs, NJ: Prentice Hall.

Bankole, K. O. (2006). A preliminary report and commentary on the structure of graduate Afrocentric research and implications for the advancement of the discipline of Africalogy, 1980–2004. *Journal of Black Studies, 36*(5), 663–697.

Banks, W. (1976). White preference in Blacks: A paradigm in search of a phenomenon. *Psychological Bulletin, 83*(6), 1179–1186. doi:10.1037/0033-2909.83.6.1179

Banks, W., Stitt, K. R., Curtis, H. A., & McQuater, G. V. (1977). Perceived objectivity and the effects of evaluative reinforcement upon compliance and self-evaluation in Blacks. *Journal of Experimental Social Psychology, 13*(5), 452–463. doi:10.1016/0022-1031(77)90030-0

Beady, C. H., & Hansell, S. (1981). Teacher race and expectations for student achievement. *American Educational Research Journal, 18*(2), 191–206.

Bergin, D. A., & Cooks, H. C. (2002). High school students of color talk about accusations of "acting White." *The Urban Review, 34*(2), 113–134.

Betancourt, H., & Lopez, S. R. (1993). The study of culture, ethnicity, and race in American psychology. *American Psychologist, 48*(6), 629–637.

Blascovich, J., Spencer, S. J., Quinn, D., & Steele, C. (2001). African Americans and high blood pressure: The role of stereotype threat. *Psychological Science, 12*(3), 225–229. doi:10.1111/1467-9280.00340

Bonilla-Silva, E. (2006). *Racism without racists: Color-blind racism and the persistence of racial inequality in the United States.* Lanham, MD: Rowman & Littlefield Publishers.

Boykin, A. W. (1983). The academic performance of Afro-American children. In J. Spence (Ed.), *Achievement and achievement motives* (pp. 321–371). San Francisco, CA: W. Freeman.

Boykin, A. W. (1986). The triple quandary and the schooling of Afro-American children. In U. Neisser (Ed.), *The school achievement of minority children* (pp. 57–92). Hillsdale, NJ: Erlbaum.

Boykin, A. W., & Allen, B. A. (1988). Rhythmic movement facilitation of learning in working-class Afro-American children. *The Journal of Genetic Psychology, 149*, 335–347.

Boykin, A. W., & Cunningham, R. (2001). The effects of movement expressiveness in story content and learning context on the analogical reasoning performance of African American children. *Journal of Negro Education, 70*(1–2), 72–83.

Boykin, A. W., & Toms, F. D. (1985). *Black child socialization: A conceptual framework.* In H. P. McAdoo & J. L. McAdoo (Eds.), *Black children: Social, educational and parental environments* (pp. 33–52). Beverly Hills: Sage.

Bradley, M. (1991). *The iceman inheritance: Prehistoric sources of western man's racism, sexism and aggression.* New York, NY: Kayode Publications.

Brown, B., Lohr, M. J., & McClenahan, E. L. (1986). Early adolescents' perceptions of peer pressure. *The Journal of Early Adolescence, 6*(2), 139–154.

Brown v. Board of Education, 347 U.S. 483 (1954). Record Group 21, Records of the U.S. District Court of Kansas, National Archives–Central Plains Region, Kansas City, MO.

Burdman, P. (2003). Investigating below the surface. *Black Issues in Higher Education, 20*, 30–33. Interview with John Ogbu.

Carney, D. R., Jost, J. T., Gosling, S. D., & Potter, J. (2008). The secret lives of liberals and conservatives: Personality profiles, interaction styles, and the things they leave behind. *Political Psychology, 29*(6), 807–840. doi:10.1111/j.1467-9221.2008.00668.x

Carr, P. B., & Steele, C. M. (2009). Stereotype threat and inflexible perseverance in problem solving. *Journal of Experimental Social Psychology, 45*(4), 853–859. doi:10.1016/j.jesp.2009.03.003

Carter, R. T. (1995). *The influence of race and racial identity in psychotherapy: Toward a racially inclusive model.* New York, NY: John Wiley & Sons, Inc.

Charles, C. Z., & Torres, K. C. (2004). Ogbu can't see the forest or the trees. *Psych Critiques, 49*(Suppl. 14).

Chavous, T. M., Bernat, D., Schmeelk-Cone, K., Caldwell, C. H., Kohn-Wood, L., & Zimmerman, M. A. (2003). Racial identity and academic attainment among African American adolescents. *Child Development, 74*(4), 1076–1090.

Cheng, S., & Starks, B. (2002). Racial differences in the effects of significant others on students' educational expectations. *Sociology of Education, 75*(4), 306–327. doi:10.2307/3090281

Childers, S. M. (2011). Getting in trouble: Feminist postcritical policy ethnography in an urban school. *Qualitative Inquiry, 17*(4), 345–354.

Chua, A. (2011). *Battle hymn of the tiger mother.* Bloomsbury Publishing.

Clark, K. B., & Clark, M. P. (1947). Racial identification and preferences in Negro children. *Personality and Social Psychology Bulletin, 5*, 420–437.

Clarke, J. H. (1999). *My life in search of Africa.* Chicago, IL: Third World Press.

Clasen, D. R., & Brown, B. (1985). The multidimensionality of peer pressure in adolescence. *Journal of Youth and Adolescence, 14*(6), 451–468.

Claveria, J. G., & Alonso, J. G. (2003). Why Roma do not like mainstream schools: Voices of a people without territory. *Harvard Educational Review, 73*, 559–590.

Cohen, G. L., Steele, C. M., & Ross, L. D. (1999). The mentor's dilemma: Providing critical feedback across the racial divide. *Personality and Social Psychology Bulletin, 25*(10), 1302–1318. doi:10.1177/0146167299258011

Cokley, K. (2000). An investigation of academic self-concept and its relationship to academic achievement in African American college students. *Journal of Black Psychology, 26*(2), 148–164. doi:10.1177/0095798400026002002

Cokley, K. O. (2001). Gender differences among African American students in the impact of racial identity on academic psychosocial development. *Journal of College Student Development, 42*(5), 480–487.

Cokley, K. O. (2002a). Ethnicity, gender and academic self-concept: A preliminary examination of academic disidentification and implications for psychologists. *Cultural Diversity and Ethnic Minority Psychology, 8*(4), 378–388. doi:10.1037/1099-9809.8.4.379

Cokley, K. O. (2002b). Testing Cross's revised racial identity model: An examination of the relationship between racial identity and internalized racialism. *Journal of Counseling Psychology, 49*, 476–483.

Cokley, K. O. (2003). What do we know about the motivation of African American students? Challenging the "anti-intellectual" myth. *Harvard Educational Review*, 73(4), 524–558.

Cokley, K. O. (2005). Racial(ized) identity, ethnic identity, and Afrocentric values: Conceptual and methodological challenges in understanding African American identity. *Journal of Counseling Psychology*, 52, 517–526.

Cokley, K. (2009). Teaching about the psychology of race and racism: Lessons learned. In D. Cleveland (Ed.), *When minorities are strongly encouraged to apply: diversity and affirmative action in higher education* (pp. 147–155). New York, NY: Peter Lang Publishing.

Cokley, K. (2013). Deconstructing Ogbu's acting White thesis: An Africentric critique. *Texas Education Review*, 1, 154–163.

Cokley, K., & Chapman, C. (2008). The roles of ethnic identity, anti-White attitudes, and academic self-concept in African American student achievement. *Social Psychology of Education: An International Journal*, 11, 349–365.

Cokley, K., & Chapman, C. (2009). Racial identity theory: Adults. In H. Neville, B. Tynes, & S. Utsey (Eds.), *Handbook of African American psychology* (pp. 283–298). Thousand Oaks, CA: Sage Publishers.

Cokley, K., McClain, S., Jones, M., & Johnson, S. (2011). A preliminary examination of academic disidentification, racial identity, and academic achievement among African American adolescents. *The High School Journal*, 95, 54–68.

Cokley, K., & Moore, P. (2007). Moderating and mediating effects of gender and psychological disengagement on the academic achievement of African American college students. *Journal of Black Psychology*, 33, 169–187.

Constantine, M. G., Smith, L., Redington, R. M., & Owens, D. (2008). Racial microaggressions against Black counseling and counseling psychology faculty: A central challenge in the multicultural counseling movement. *Journal of Counseling & Development*, 86(3), 348–355. doi:10.1002/j.1556-6678.2008.tb00519.x

Conyers, J. L. (2004). The evolution of Africology: An Afrocentric appraisal. *Journal of Black Studies*, 34(5), 640–652.

Cook, P. J., & Ludwig, J. (1998). The burden of "acting White": Do Black adolescents disparage academic achievement? In C. Jencks and M. Phillips (Eds.), *The Black-White test score gap* (pp. 375–400). Washington, DC: Brookings Institution Press.

Coon, H. M., & Kemmelmeier, M. (2001). Cultural orientations in the United States: (Re) Examining differences among ethnic groups. *Journal of Cross-Cultural Psychology*, 32, 348–364.

Cross, W. E., Jr. (1971). The Negro-to-Black conversion experience: Toward a psychology of Black liberation. *Black World*, 20, 13–27.

Cross, W. E., Jr. (1991). *Shades of Black*. Philadelphia, PA: Temple University Press.

Cross, W. E., Jr., & Vandiver, B. J. (2001). Nigrescence theory and measurement: Introducing the Cross Racial Identity Scale (CRIS). In J. G. Ponterotto, J. M. Casas, L. A. Suzuki, & C. M. Alexander (Eds.), *Handbook of multicultural counseling* (2nd ed., pp. 371–393). Thousand Oaks, CA: Sage Publishers.

DePalma, A. (1990, November 4). The culture question. *The New York Times*.

Demo, D. H., & Parker, K. D. (1987). Academic achievement and self-esteem among Black and White college students. *Journal of Social Psychology*, 127, 345–355.

Diop, C. A. (1974). *The African origin of civilization: Myth or reality.* Chicago, IL: Lawrence Hill Books.

Eccleston, C. P., Smyth, J. M., & Lopoo, L. M. (2010). Unraveling the race paradox of achievement and self-views. *Social Psychology of Education, 13*(1), 1–18. doi:10.1007/s11218-009-9106-2

Elion, A. A., Wang, K. T., Slaney, R. B., & French, B. H. (2012). Perfectionism in African American students: Relationship to racial identity, GPA, self-esteem, and depression. *Cultural Diversity and Ethnic Minority Psychology, 18*(2), 118–127.

Ellison, C. M., Boykin, A., Tyler, K. M., & Dillihunt, M. L. (2005). Examining classroom learning preferences among elementary school students. *Social Behavior and Personality, 33*(7), 699–708. doi:10.2224/sbp.2005.33.7.699

Ferguson, R. F. (1998). Teachers' perception and expectations and the Black-White test score gap. In C. Jencks & M. Phillips (Eds.), *The Black-White test score gap* (pp. 273–317). Washington, DC: Brookings Institution Press.

Ferguson, R. F. (2003). Teachers' perceptions and expectations and the Black-White test score gap. *Urban Education, 38*(4), 460–507.

Finn, J. D. (1989). Withdrawing from school. *Review of Educational Research, 59*(2), 117–142. doi:10.2307/1170412

Flynn, F. J. (2005). Having an open mind: The impact of openness to experience on interracial attitudes and impression formation. *Journal of Personality and Social Psychology, 88*(5), 816–826. doi:10.1037/0022-3514.88.5.816

Foley, D. (2004). Ogbu's theory of academic disengagement: Its evolution and its critics. *Intercultural Education, 15,* 385–397.

Fordham, S. (1988). Racelessness as a factor in Black students' school success: Pragmatic strategy or Pyrrhic victory? *Harvard Educational Review, 58*(1), 54–85.

Fordham, S. (1996). *Blacked out: Dilemmas of race, identity, and success at Capital High.* Chicago: University of Chicago Press.

Fordham, S. (2004). "Signithia, you can do better than that": John Ogbu (and me) and the Nine Lives people. *Anthropology and Education Quarterly, 35*(1), 149–161.

Fordham, S. (2008). Beyond Capital High: On dual citizenship and the strange career of "acting White." *Anthropology and Education Quarterly, 39*(3), 227–246. doi:10.1111/j.1548-1492.2008.00019.x

Fordham, S., & Ogbu, J. U. (1986). Black students' school success: Coping with the "burden of acting White." *Urban Review, 18,* 176–206.

Foster, K. M. (2004). Coming to terms: A discussion of John Ogbu's cultural-ecological theory of minority academic achievement. *Intercultural Education, 15,* 369–384.

Frisby, C. L. (1993). One giant step backward: Myths of Black cultural learning styles. *School Psychology Review, 22*(3), 535–557.

Fulkerson, K. F., Furr, S. R., & Brown, D. (1983). Expectations and achievement among third-, sixth-, and ninth-grade Black and White males and females. *Developmental Psychology, 19*(2), 231–236. doi:10.1037/0012-1649.19.2.231

Gaines, S. R., Larbie, J., Patel, S., Pereira, L., & Sereke-Melake, Z. (2005). Cultural values among African-descended persons in the United Kingdom: Comparisons with European-descended and Asian-descended persons. *Journal of Black Psychology, 31*(2), 130–151. doi:10.1177/0095798405274720

Garibaldi, A. M. (2007). The educational status of African American males in the 21st century. *Journal of Negro Education, 76*(3), 324–333.

Gates, H. L., Jr. (1992, July 20). Black demagogues and pseudo-scholars. *The New York Times, 20,* 126–28.

Gay, G. (2002). Preparing for culturally responsive teaching. *Journal of Teacher Education, 53*(2), 106–116.

Giannino, S. S., & Campbell, S. B. (2012). The reality of the gaze: A critical discourse analysis of *Flavor of Love. International Journal of Humanities and Social Sciences, 2*(3), 59–68.

Goff, P. A., Steele, C. M., & Davies, P. G. (2008). The space between us: Stereotype threat and distance in interracial contexts. *Journal of Personality and Social Psychology, 94*(1), 91.

Gordon, D. M., Iwamoto, D. K., Ward, N., Potts, R., & Boyd, E. (2009). Mentoring urban Black middle school male students: Implications for academic achievement. *Journal of Negro Education, 78*(3), 277–289.

Graham, A., & Anderson, K. A. (2008). "I have to be three steps ahead": Academically gifted African American male students in an urban high school on the tension between an ethnic and academic identity. *The Urban Review, 40*(5), 472–499.

Graham, S. (1994). Motivation in African Americans. *Review of Educational Research, 64*(1), 55–117. doi:10.2307/1170746

Graham, S. (1997). Using attribution theory to understand social and academic motivation in African American youth. *Educational Psychologist, 32*(1), 21–34. doi:10.1207/s15326985ep3201_2

Graham, S., Taylor, A. Z., & Hudley, C. (1998). Exploring achievement values among ethnic minority early adolescents. *Journal of Educational Psychology, 90*(4), 606.

Gray, C. C. (2001). *Afrocentric thought and praxis: An intellectual history.* Trenton, NJ: Africa World Press.

Gray-Little, B., & Hafdahl, A. R. (2000). Factors influencing racial comparisons of self-esteem: A quantitative review. *Psychological Bulletin, 126*(1), 26.

Griffin, B. W. (2002). Academic disidentification, race, and high school dropouts. *The High School Journal, 85*(4), 71–81.

Gross, B., Booker, T., & Goldhaber, D. (2009). Boosting student achievement: The effect of comprehensive school reform on student achievement. *Educational Evaluation and policy Analysis, 31*(2), 111–126. doi:10.3102/0162373709333886

Gumora, G., & Arsenio, W. F. (2002). Emotionality, emotional regulation, and school performance in middle school children. *Journal of School Psychology, 40,* 395–413.

Hale, J. E. (1993). Rejoinder to "... Myths of Black cultural learning styles" in defence of Afrocentric scholarship. *School Psychology Review, 22*(3), 558–561.

Hale-Benson, J. (1986). *Black children: Their roots, culture, and learning styles.* Baltimore, MD: Johns Hopkins University Press.

Hamlet, J. D. (1998). *Afrocentric visions: studies in culture and communication.* Thousand Oaks, CA: Sage Publishers.

Harlow, R. (2003). "Race doesn't matter, but ...": The effect of race on professors' experiences and emotion management in the undergraduate college classroom. *Social Psychology Quarterly, 66,* 348–363.

Harper, B. E. (2010). Show and prove: Investigating differences in the self-beliefs of Black and White honor students. *Social Psychology of Education, 13*(4), 473–483. doi:10.1007/s11218-010-9122-2

Harper, B. E., & Tuckman, B. W. (2006). Racial identity beliefs and academic achievement: Does being Black hold students back? *Social Psychology of Education, 9,* 381–403.

Harris, A. L. (2011). *Kids don't want to fail: Oppositional culture and the Black-White achievement gap.* Cambridge, MA: Harvard University Press.

Harris, A. L., & Robinson, K. (2007). Schooling behaviors or prior skills? A cautionary tale of omitted variable bias within oppositional culture theory. *Sociology of Education, 80*(2), 139–157. doi:10.1177/003804070708000203

Helms, J. E. (Ed.) (1990). *Black and White racial identity: Theory, research, and practice.* Westport, CT: Greenwood Press.

Helms, J. E. (1992). Why is there no study of cultural equivalence in standardized cognitive ability testing? *American Psychologist, 47*(9), 1083–1101.

Helms, J. E., & Cook, D. A. (1999). *Using race and culture in counseling and psychotherapy: Theory and process.* Needham Heights, MA: Allyn & Bacon.

Helms, J. E., Malone, I., S., Henze, K., Satiani, A., Perry, J., & Warren, A. (2003). First annual diversity challenge. "How to survive teaching courses on race and culture." *Journal of Multicultural Counseling and Development, 31*, 3–11.

Helms, J. E., & Parham, T. A. (1990). Racial Identity Attitude Scale. In R. L. Jones (Ed.), *Handbook of Tests and Measurements.* Richmond, CA: Cobb and Henry.

Helms, J. E., & Parham, T. A. (1996). The development of the Racial Identity Attitude Scale. In R. L. Jones (Ed.), *Handbook of Tests and Measurements for Black Populations.* Vol. 2 (pp. 167–174). Hampton, VA: Cobb & Henry.

Henry, G. T., Fortner, C., & Thompson, C. L. (2010). Targeted funding for educationally disadvantaged students: A regression discontinuity estimate of the impact on high school student achievement. *Educational Evaluation And Policy Analysis, 32*(2), 183–204. doi:10.3102/0162373710370620

Herrnstein, R., & Murray, C. (1994). *The bell curve.* New York, NY: Free Press.

Hilliard, A. G., III (1976). *Alternatives to IQ testing: An approach to the identification of gifted minority children (final report).* San Francisco, CA: San Francisco State University. (ERIC Document Reproduction Service No. ED 103067).

Holloway, J. E. (1990). *Africanisms in American culture.* Bloomington, IN: Indiana University Press.

Howe, S. (1998). *Afrocentrism: Mythical pasts and imagined homes.* New York, NY: Verso Publishers.

Inzlicht, M., & Kang, S. K. (2010). Stereotype threat spillover: How coping with threats to social identity affects aggression, eating, decision making, and attention. *Journal of Personality and Social Psychology, 99*(3), 467–481. doi:10.1037/a0018951

Irvine, J. J. (1990). *Black students and school failure: Policies, practices, and prescriptions.* Westport, CT: Greenwood Press.

Jackson, L. C. (1999). Ethnocultural resistance to multicultural training: Students and faculty. *Cultural Diversity & Ethnic Minority Psychology, 5*(1), 27–36.

Jencks, C. & Phillips, M. (Eds.). (1998). *The Black-White test score gap.* Washington, DC: Brookings Institution Press.

Jensen, A. (1973). *Educability and group differences.* New York, NY: Harper & Row.

Johnson, R. (1993). Factors in the academic success of African American college males. *Dissertation Abstracts International, 54*, 1696.

Kambon, K. K. (1998). *African/Black psychology in the American context: An African-centered approach.* Tallahassee, FL: Nubian Nation Publications.

Kambon, K. K. (2004). The worldviews paradigm as the conceptual framework for African/Black psychology. In R. Jones (Ed.), *Black psychology.* Hampton, VA: Cobb & Henry.

Kao, G., & Tienda, M. (1998). Educational aspirations of minority youth. *American Journal of Education, 106*(3), 349–384. doi:10.1086/444188

Karenga, M. (2002). *Introduction to Black studies*. Los Angeles, CA: University of Sankore Press.

Keita, M. (2000). *Race and the writing of history: Riddling the sphinx*. Oxford, UK: Oxford University Press.

Klopfenstein, K. (2005). Beyond test scores: The impact of Black teacher role models on rigorous math taking. *Contemporary Economic Policy, 23*(3), 416–428.

Komarraju, M., & Cokley, K. O. (2008). Horizontal and vertical dimensions of individualism-collectivism: A comparison of African Americans and European Americans. *Cultural Diversity and Ethnic Minority Psychology, 14*(4), 336–343. doi:10.1037/1099-9809.14.4.336

Kurtz-Costes, B., Ehrlich, M., McCall, R. J., & Loridant, C. (1995). Motivational determinants of reading comprehension: A comparison of French, Caucasian-American, and African-American adolescents. *Applied Cognitive Psychology, 9*(4), 351–364. doi:10.1002/acp.2350090407

Kwadwo (Ed.) (2000). *To be African: Essays by some of the great thinkers of our time*. Unpublished book manuscript.

Ladson-Billings, G. (1995). But that's just good teaching! The case for culturally relevant pedagogy. *Theory into Practice, 34*(3), 159–165.

Ladson-Billings, G. (2007). Pushing past the achievement gap: An essay on the language of deficit. *Journal of Negro Education, 76*(3), 316–323.

Lay, R., & Wakstein, J. (1985). Race, academic achievement, and self-concept of ability. *Research in Higher Education, 22*, 43–64.

Lee, S., Juon, H., Martinez, G., Hsu, C. E., Robinson, E., Bawa, J., & Ma, G. X. (2009). Model minority at risk: Expressed needs of mental health by Asian American young adults. *Journal of Community Health: The Publication for Health Promotion and Disease Prevention, 34*(2), 144–152. doi:10.1007/s10900-008-9137-1

Lefkowitz, M. (1996). *Not out of Africa: How "Afrocentrism" became an excuse to teach myth as history*. New York, NY: Basic Books.

Lehman, B. (2012). The impacts of friendship groups' racial composition when perceptions of prejudice threaten students' academic self-concept. *Social Psychology of Education, 15*(3), 411–425. doi:10.1007/s11218-012-9190-6

Lent, R. W., Brown, S. D., & Gore, P. R. (1997). Discriminant and predictive validity of academic self-concept, academic self-efficacy, and mathematics-specific self-efficacy. *Journal of Counseling Psychology, 44*(3), 307–315. doi:10.1037/0022-0167.44.3.307

Leung, A. Y., & Chiu, C. (2008). Interactive effects of multicultural experiences and openness to experience on creative potential. *Creativity Research Journal, 20*(4), 376–382. doi:10.1080/10400410802391371

Lockett, C. T., & Harrell, J. P. (2003). Racial identity, self-esteem, and academic achievement: Too much interpretation, too little supporting data. *Journal of Black Psychology, 29*, 325–336.

Lovejoy, P. E. (2005). *The "Middle Passage": The enforced migration of Africans across the Atlantic*. Ann Arbor, MI: ProQuest Information and Learning.

Lundy, F. G. (2003). The myths of oppositional culture. *Journal of Black Studies, 33*, 450–467.

Major, B., & Schmader, T. (1998). Coping with stigma through psychological disengagement. In J. Swim & C. Stangor (Eds.), *Prejudice: The target's perspective* (pp. 219–241). New York, NY: Academic.

Majors, R., & Billson, J. (1992). *Cool pose: The dilemmas of Black manhood in America.* New York, NY: Lexington.

Marryshow, D., Hurley, E. A., Allen, B. A., Tyler, K. M., & Boykin, A. (2005). Impact of learning orientation on African American children's attitudes toward high-achieving peers. *The American Journal of Psychology, 118*(4), 603–618.

Marsh, H. W., & Craven, R. G. (2006). Reciprocal effects of self-concept and performance from a multidimensional perspective: Beyond seductive pleasure and unidimensional perspectives. *Perspectives on Psychological Science, 1*(2), 133–163. doi:10.1111/j.1745-6916.2006.00010.x

Marsh, H. W., & Martin, A. J. (2011). Academic self-concept and academic achievement: Relations and causal ordering. *British Journal of Educational Psychology, 81*(1), 59–77. doi:10.1348/000709910X503501

Marsh, H. W., & O'Mara, A. (2008). Reciprocal effects between academic self-concept, self-esteem, achievement, and attainment over seven adolescent years: Unidimensional and multidimensional perspectives of self-concept. *Personality and Social Psychology Bulletin, 34*(4), 542–552. doi:10.1177/0146167207312313

Martinez, R. O., & Dukes, R. L. (1997). The effects of ethnic identity, ethnicity, and gender on adolescent well-being. *Journal of Youth and Adolescence, 26*(5), 503–516. doi:10.1023/A:1024525821078

Mazama, A. (2001). The Afrocentric paradigm: Contours and definitions. *Journal of Black Studies, 31,* 387–405.

Mazama, A. (Ed.) (2003). *The Afrocentric paradigm.* Trenton, NJ: Africa World Press.

McAbee, S. T., & Oswald, F. L. (2013). The criterion-related validity of personality measures for predicting GPA: A meta-analytic validity competition. *Psychological Assessment, 25*(2), 532–544. doi:10.1037/a0031748

McAdoo, H. P., & McAdoo, J. L. (Eds.). (1985). *Black children: Social, educational and parental environments.* Beverly Hills, CA: Sage.

McGowan, J. M. (2000). Multicultural teaching: African American faculty classroom teaching experiences in predominantly White colleges and universities. *Multicultural Education, 8,* 19–22.

McKown, C., & Weinstein, R. S. (2008). Teacher expectations, classroom context, and the achievement gap. *Journal of School Psychology, 46*(3), 235–261.

McWhorter, J. (2000). *Losing the race: Self-sabotage in Black America.* New York, NY: Free Press.

Mintz, S. W., & Price, R. (1992). *The birth of African-American culture.* Boston, MA: Beacon Press:

Morgan, S. L., & Mehta, J. D. (2004). Beyond the laboratory: Evaluating the survey evidence for the disidentification explanation of Black-White differences in achievement. *Sociology of Education, 77*(1), 82–101.

Mruk, C. (2013). *Self-esteem and positive psychology.* New York, NY: Springer Publishing Company.

Murphy-Shigematsu, S., Sein, K., Wakimoto, P., & Wang, M. (2012). Asian American student stress: The other side of achievement. In E. Shrake & E. Chen (Eds.), *Asian Pacific American experiences: Past, present, and future* (pp. 204–219). Dubuque, IA: Kendall Hunt Publishing Company

Murrell, P. C. (2002). *African-centered pedagogy: Developing schools of achievement for African American children.* Albany, NY: State University of New York Press.

Myers, L. J. (1988). *Understanding an Afrocentric Worldview: Introduction to an optimal psychology*. Dubuque, IA: Kendall Hunt Publishing Company.

Nasir, N., McLaughlin, M. W., & Jones, A. (2009). What does it mean to be African American? Constructions of race and academic identity in an urban public high school. *American Educational Research Journal, 46*(1), 73–114.

Neblett, E. R., Philip, C. L., Cogburn, C. D., & Sellers, R. M. (2006). African American adolescents' discrimination experiences and academic achievement: Racial socialization as a cultural compensatory and protective factor. *Journal of Black Psychology, 32*(2), 199–218. doi:10.1177/0095798406287072

Nobles, W. W. (1972). African philosophy: Foundations for Black psychology. In R. Jones (Ed.), *Black psychology* (pp. 18–32). New York, NY; Harper & Row.

Nobles, W. W. (1974). African root, American fruit: The Black family. *Journal of Social and Behavioral Sciences, 20*, 52–63.

Nobles, W. W. (1985). *Africanity and the Black family: The development of a theoretical model*. Oakland, CA: Black Family Institute Publications.

Nobles, W. W. (1986). *African psychology: Toward its reclamation, reascension and revitalization*. Oakland, CA: Black Family Institute Publications.

Nobles, W. W. (2000). To be African. In Kwadwo (Ed.), *To be African: Essays by some of the great thinkers of our time*. Unpublished book manuscript.

Noftle, E. E., & Robins, R. W. (2007). Personality predictors of academic outcomes: Big five correlates of GPA and SAT scores. *Journal of Personality and Social Psychology, 93*(1), 116–130.

O'Brien, E. J., Bartoletti, M., & Leitzel, J. D. (2006). Self-esteem, psychopathology and psychotherapy. In M. Kernis (Ed.), *Self-esteem issues and answers: A source book of current perspectives*. New York, NY: Psychology Press.

Ogbu, J. U. (1981). Origins of human competence: A cultural-ecological perspective. *Child Development, 52*(2), 413–429.

Ogbu, J. U. (2004). Collective identity and the burden of "acting White" in Black History, community, and education. *The Urban Review, 36*, 1–35.

Ogbu, J. U., & Simons, F. (1988). *Black autobiographies: A search for cultural model of minority status and American society*. Unpublished manuscript. Survey Research Center, University of California, Berkeley, CA.

Osborne, J. W. (1995). Academics, self-esteem, and race: A look at the underlying assumptions of the disidentification hypothesis. *Personality and Social Psychology Bulletin, 21*(5), 449–455. doi:10.1177/0146167295215003

Osborne, J. W. (1997). Race and academic disidentification. *Journal of Educational Psychology, 89*(4), 728–735. doi:10.1037/0022-0663.89.4.728

Osborne, J. W. (1999). Unraveling underachievement among African American boys from an identification with academics perspective. *Journal of Negro Education, 68*(4), 555–565.

Oyserman, D., Bybee, D., & Terry, K. (2003). Gendered racial identity and involvement with school. *Self and Identity, 2*, 307–324.

Oyserman, D., Coon, H. M., & Kemmelmeier, M. (2002). Rethinking individualism and collectivism: Evaluation of theoretical assumptions and meta-analyses. *Psychological Bulletin, 128*, 3–72.

Oyserman, D., Harrison, K., & Bybee, D. (2001). Can racial identity be promotive of academic efficacy? *International Journal of Behavioral Development, 25*(4), 379–385. doi:10.1080/01650250042000401

Oyserman, D., Kemmelmeier, M., Fryberg, S., Brosh, H., & Hart-Johnson, T. (2003). Racial-ethnic self-schemas. *Social Psychology Quarterly, 66,* 333–347.

Parham, T. A. (1989). Cycles of psychological nigrescence. *The Counseling Psychologist, 17,* 187–226.

Parham, T. A. (1997). *Psychological storms: The African American struggle for identity.* Sauk Village, IL: African American Images.

Parham, T. A. (2002). *Counseling persons of African descent.* Thousand Oaks, CA: Sage Publications.

Parham, T. A., Ajamu, A., & White, J. (2010). *Psychology of Blacks: Centering our perspectives in African consciousness* (4th ed.). Upper Saddle River, NJ: Pearson.

Parham, T. A., & Helms, J. E. (1981). The influence of Black students' racial identity attitudes on preference for counselor's race. *Journal of Counseling Psychology, 28,* 250–258.

Parham, T. A., & Helms, J. E. (1985). Attitudes of racial identity and self-esteem of Black students: An exploratory investigation. *Journal of College Student Personnel, 26*(2), 143–147.

Peters, E. (1994). Afrocentricity: Problematics of method and nomenclature. Working Papers in African American Studies. University of Notre Dame.

Peters, E. (2001). Afrocentricity: Problematics of method and nomenclature. In N. Norment Jr. (Ed.), *The African American studies reader.* Durham, NC: Carolina Academic Press.

Phinney, J. S. (1990). Ethnic identity in adolescents and adults: Review of research. *Psychological Bulletin, 108,* 499–514.

Phinney, J. S. (1992). The Multigroup Ethnic Identity Measure. *Journal of Adolescent Research, 7,* 156–176.

Phinney, J. S. (1996). When we talk about American ethnic groups, what do we mean? *American Psychologist, 51,* 918–927.

Pittman, C. T. (2010). Race and gender oppression in the classroom: The experiences of women faculty of color with White male students. *Teaching Sociology, 38,* 183–196.

Pittman, C. T. (2012). Racial microaggressions: The narratives of African American faculty at a predominantly White university. *Journal of Negro Education, 81*(1), 82–92.

Pollard, D., & Ajirotutu, C. (Eds.). (2000). *African-centered schooling in theory and practice.* Westport, CT: Greenwood Publishing Group.

Radziwon, C. (2003). The effects of peers' beliefs on 8th-grade students' identification with school. *Journal of Research in Childhood Education, 17*(2), 236–249.

Ransby, B. (2000). Afrocentrism, cultural nationalism, and the problem with essentialist definitions of race, gender and sexuality. In M. Marable (Ed.), *Dispatches from the Ivory Tower.* New York, NY: Columbia University Press.

Restall, M. (2000). Black conquistadors: Armed Africans in early Spanish America. *The Americas, 57*(2), 171–205.

Reynolds, W. M. (1988). Measurement of academic self-concept in college students. *Journal of Personality Assessment, 52*(2), 223–240. doi:10.1207/s15327752jpa5202_4

Richardson, T. Q. (1993). Black cultural learning styles: Is it really a myth? *School Psychology Review, 22*(3), 562–567.

Rivers, S. (2010). Sankofa Shule (Lansing, Michigan). In K. Lomotey (Ed.), *Encyclopedia of African American Education* (Vol. 1., pp. 558–560). Thousand Oaks, CA: Sage.

Rogers, J. A. (1996). *World's great men of color.* New York, NY: Touchstone.

Rosenberg, M., & Simmons, R. (1972). *Black and White self-esteem: The urban school child* (Rose Monograph Series). Washington, DC: American Sociological Association.

Ross, S. I., & Jackson, J. M. (1991). Teachers' expectations for Black males' and Black females' academic achievement. *Personality and Social Psychology Bulletin, 17*(1), 78–82.

Rowley, S. J., Sellers, R. M., Chavous, T. M., & Smith, M. A. (1998). The relationship between racial identity and self-esteem in African American college and high school students. *Journal of Personality and Social Psychology, 74*(3), 715–724.

Rubovits, P. C., & Maehr, M. L. (1973). Pygmalion black and white. *Journal of Personality and Social Psychology, 25*(2), 210.

Rumberger, R. W., & Palardy, G. J. (2005). Does segregation still matter? The impact of student composition on academic achievement in high school. *Teachers College Record, 107*(9), 1999–2045. doi:10.1111/j.1467-9620.2005.00583.x

Rushton, J. P. (1997). *Race, evolution, and behavior: A life history perspective.* New Brunswick, NJ: Transaction.

Rushton, J., & Jensen, A. R. (2005). Thirty years of research on race differences in cognitive ability. *Psychology, Public Policy, and Law, 11*(2), 235–294. doi:10.1037/1076-8971.11.2.235

Ryan, R. M., & Deci, E. L. (2000). Self-determination theory and the facilitation of intrinsic motivation, social development, and well-being. *American Psychologist, 55*(1), 68–78. doi:10.1037/0003-066X.55.1.68

Schmader, T., Johns, M., & Forbes, C. (2008). An integrated process model of stereotype threat effects on performance. *Psychological Review, 115*(2), 336–356. doi:10.1037/0033-295X.115.2.336

Schmader, T., Major, B., & Gramzow, R. W. (2001). Coping with ethnic stereotypes in the academic domain: Perceived injustice and psychological disengagement. *Journal of Social Issues, 57*(1), 93–111.

Seaton, E. K., Caldwell, C. H., Sellers, R. M., & Jackson, J. S. (2008). The prevalence of perceived discrimination among African American and Caribbean Black youth. *Developmental Psychology, 44*(5), 1288–1297. doi:10.1037/a0012747

Seaton, E. K., Caldwell, C. H., Sellers, R. M., & Jackson, J. S. (2010). An intersectional approach for understanding perceived discrimination and psychological well-being among African American and Caribbean Black youth. *Developmental Psychology, 46*(5), 1372–1379. doi:10.1037/a0019869

Sellers, R. M., Chavous, T. M., & Cooke, D. Y. (1998). Racial ideology and racial centrality as predictors of African American college students' academic performance. *Journal of Black Psychology, 24*, 8–27.

Sellers, R. M., Rowley, S. J., Chavous, T. M., Shelton, J., & Smith, M. A. (1997). Multidimensional Inventory of Black Identity: A preliminary investigation of reliability and construct validity. *Journal of Personality and Social Psychology, 73*(4), 805–815. doi:10.1037/0022-3514.73.4.805.

Sellers, R. M., Smith, M. A., Shelton, J. N., Rowley, S. A., & Chavous, T. M. (1998). Multidimensional model of racial identity: A reconceptualization of African-American racial identity. *Personality and Social Psychology Review, 2*, 18–39.

Semmes, C. E. (1981). Foundations of an Afrocentric social science: Implications for curriculum building, theory, and research in Black studies. *Journal of Black Studies, 12*(1),
3–17.

Shavelson, R. J., & Bolus, R. (1982). Self concept: The interplay of theory and methods.
Journal of Educational Psychology, 74(1), 3–17. doi:10.1037/0022-0663.74.1.3

Shockley, K. (2011). Reaching African American students: Profile of an Afrocentric
teacher. *Journal of Black Studies, 42*(7), 1027–1046. doi:10.1177/0021934711403739

Shockley, K. G. (2007). Literatures and definitions: Toward understanding Africentric
education. *Journal of Negro Education, 76*(2), 103–117.

Shockley, K. G., & Frederick, R. M. (2010). Constructs and dimensions of Afrocentric
education. *Journal of Black Studies, 40*(6), 1212–1233. doi:10.1177/002193
4708325517

Shujaa, M. (2003). Education and schooling: You can have one without the other.
In A. Mazama (Ed.), *The Afrocentric paradigm* (pp. 245–264). Trenton, NJ: Africa
World Press.

Sibley, C. G., & Duckitt, J. (2008). Personality and prejudice: A meta-analysis and theoretical review. *Personality and Social Psychology Review, 12*(3), 248–279. doi:10.1177/
1088868308319226

Sibley, C. G., Osborne, D., & Duckitt, J. (2012). Personality and political orientation:
Meta-analysis and test of a threat-constraint model. *Journal of Research in Personality,
46*(6), 664–677. doi:10.1016/j.jrp.2012.08.002

Sirin, S. R. (2005). Socioeconomic status and academic achievement: A meta-analytic
review of research. *Review of Educational Research, 75*(3), 417–453.

Slavin, R. E., & Oickle, E. (1981). Effects of cooperative learning teams on student
achievement and race relations: Treatment by race interactions. *Sociology of
Education, 54*, 174–180.

Soberman, L. (1994). *Psychometric validation of a brief teacher screening instrument*
(Unpublished doctoral dissertation). University of Oregon, Eugene.

Soto, J. A., Dawson-Andoh, N. A., & BeLue, R. (2011). The relationship between perceived discrimination and Generalized Anxiety Disorder among African Americans,
Afro Caribbeans, and non-Hispanic Whites. *Journal of Anxiety Disorders, 25*(2),
258–265. doi:10.1016/j.janxdis.2010.09.011

Sowell, T. (1986). *Education: Assumptions versus history.* Stanford, CA: Hoover Institution
Press.

Spencer, M. B., Noll, E., Stoltzfus, J., & Harpalani, V. (2001). Identity and school adjustment: Revisiting the "Acting White" assumption. *Educational Psychologist, 36*, 21–30.

Steele, C. M. (1992). Race and the schooling of Black Americans. *Atlantic Monthly, 269*,
68–78.

Steele, C. M. (1997). A threat in the air: How stereotypes shape intellectual identity
and performance. *American Psychologist, 52*(6), 613–629. doi:10.1037/0003
-066X.52.6.613

Steele, C. M. (1998). Stereotyping and its threat are real. *American Psychologist, 53*,
680–681.

Steele, C. M. (1999). Thin ice: Stereotype threat and Black college students. *Atlantic
Monthly, 248*, 44–54.

Steele, C. M. (2010). *Whistling Vivaldi: And other clues to how stereotypes affect us (issues of
our time).* New York, NY: W. W. Norton & Company.

Steele, C. M., & Aronson, J. (1995). Stereotype threat and the intellectual test performance of African Americans. *Journal of Personality and Social Psychology*, 69(5),
797–811. doi:10.1037/0022-3514.69.5.797

Steele, S. (1991). *The content of our character: A new vision of race in America*. New York,
NY: St. Martin's Press.

Stryker, S., & Serpe, R. T. (1982). Commitment, identity salience and role behavior. In
W. Ickes & E. Knowles (Eds.), *Personality, roles, and social behavior* (pp. 199–218).
New York, NY: Springer-Verlag.

Stryker, S., & Serpe, R. T. (1994). Identity salience and psychological centrality: Equivalent, overlapping, or complementary concepts? *Social Psychology Quarterly*, 57, 16–35.

Sue, D., Capodilupo, C. M., & Holder, A. B. (2008). Racial microaggressions in the life experience of Black Americans. *Professional Psychology: Research and Practice*, 39(3), 329–336.

Sue, D., Nadal, K. L., Capodilupo, C. M., Lin, A. I., Torino, G. C., & Rivera, D. P.
(2008). Racial microaggressions against Black Americans: Implications for counseling. *Journal of Counseling & Development*, 86(3), 330–338.

Sue, S., & Okazaki, S. (1990). Asian-American educational achievements: A phenomenon in search of an explanation. *American Psychologist*, 45(8), 913–920.
doi:10.1037/0003-066X.45.8.913

Tatum, B. (1992). *"Why are all the Black kids sitting together in the cafeteria?" And other conversations about race. A psychologist explains the development of racial identity*. New York,
NY: Basic Books.

Taylor, R. D., Casten, R., Flickinger, S. M., Roberts, D., & Fulmore, C. D. (1994).
Explaining the school performance of African-American adolescents. *Journal of
Research on Adolescence*, 4(1), 21–44

Taylor, V., & Walton, G. M. (2011). Stereotype threat undermines academic learning.
Personality and Social Psychology Bulletin, 37(8), 1055–1067. doi:10.1177/
0146167211406506

Thomas, O. N., Caldwell, C., Faison, N., & Jackson, J. S. (2009). Promoting academic
achievement: The role of racial identity in buffering perceptions of teacher discrimination on academic achievement among African American and Caribbean Black adolescents. *Journal of Educational Psychology*, 101(2), 420–431. doi:10.1037/a0014578

Twenge, J. M., & Crocker, J. (2002). Race and self-esteem: Meta-analyses comparing
Whites, Blacks, Hispanics, Asians, and American Indians and comment on
Gray-Little and Hafdahl (2000). *Psychological Bulletin*, 128(3), 371–408.

Tyler, K. M., Boykin, A. W., Miller, O., & Hurley, E. (2006). Cultural values in the home
and school experiences of low-income African American students. *Social Psychology of
Education*, 9, 363–380.

Tyson, K. (2002). Weighing in: Elementary-age students and the debate on attitudes
toward school among Black students. *Social Forces*, 80(4), 1157–1189.

Tyson, K., Darity, W. R., & Castellino, D. R. (2005). It's not "a Black thing":
Understanding the burden of acting White and other dilemmas of high achievement.
American Sociological Review, 70(4), 582–605. doi:10.1177/000312240507000403

Valencia, R. R., & Suzuki, L. A. (2000). *Intelligence testing and minority students: Foundations, performance factors, and assessment issues* (Vol. 3). Thousand Oaks, CA: Sage.

Valiente, C., Swanson, J., & Eisenberg, N. (2012). Linking students' emotions and academic achievement: When and why emotions matter. *Child Development Perspectives*,
6(2), 129–135.

Vallerand, R. J., Pelletier, L. G., Blais, M. R., & Brière, N. M. (1992). The Academic Motivation Scale: A measure of intrinsic, extrinsic, and amotivation in education. *Educational and Psychological Measurement, 52*(4), 1003–1017. doi:10.1177/0013164492052004025

Vandiver, B. J., Cross, W. E., Jr., Fhagen-Smith, P. E., Worrell, F. C., Swim, J., & Caldwell, L. (2000). *The Cross Racial Identity Scale.* Unpublished scale.

Vandiver, B. J., Fhagen-Smith, P. E., Jr., Worrell, F. C., & Fhagen-Smith, P. E. (2002). Validating the Cross Racial Identity Scale. *Journal of Counseling Psychology, 49,* 71–85.

Van Laar, C. (2000). The paradox of low academic achievement but high self-esteem in African American students: An attributional account. *Educational Psychology Review, 12,* 33–60.

Vickerman, M. (2001). Tweaking a monolith: The West Indian immigrant encounter with "Blackness." In N. Foner (Ed.), *Islands in the city: West Indian migration to New York* (pp. 237–256). Los Angeles, CA: University of California Press.

Voelkl, K. E. (1997). Identification with school. *American Journal of Education, 105*(3), 294–318. doi:10.1086/444158

Whaley, A. L. (1998). Issues of validity in empirical tests of stereotype threat theory. *American Psychologist, 53,* 679–680.

White, K. R. (1982). The relation between socioeconomic status and academic achievement. *Psychological Bulletin, 91*(3), 461–481. doi:10.1037/0033-2909.91.3.461

Wildhagen, T. (2012). How teachers and schools contribute to racial differences in the realization of academic potential. *Teachers College Record, 114*(7), n7.

Willis, M. G. (1989). Learning styles of African American children: A review of the literature and interventions. *Journal of Black Psychology, 16*(1), 47–65. doi:10.1177/009579848901600105

Witherspoon, K., Speight, S. L., & Thomas, A. (1997). Racial identity attitudes, school achievement, and academic self-efficacy among African American high school students. *Journal of Black Psychology, 23*(4), 344–357.

Worrell, F. C. (2007). Ethnic identity, academic achievement, and global self-concept in four groups of academically talented adolescents. *Gifted Child Quarterly, 51,* 23–38.

Wright, B. L. (2011). I know who I am, do you? Identity and academic achievement of successful African American male adolescents in an urban pilot high school in the United States. *Urban Education, 46*(4), 611–638.

Yasui, M., Dorham, C. L., & Dishion, T. J. (2004). Ethnic identity and psychological adjustment: A validity analysis for European American and African American adolescents. *Journal of Adolescent Research, 19*(6), 807–825.

Ying, Y., Lee, P., Tsai, J. L., Hung, Y., Lin, M., & Wan, C. (2001). Asian American college students as model minorities: An examination of their overall competence. *Cultural Diversity and Ethnic Minority Psychology, 7*(1), 59–74. doi:10.1037/1099-9809.7.1.59

Ziegler, D. (1995). *Molefi Kete Asante: In praise and in criticism.* Emeryville, CA: Winston Derek Publishers.

Zuckerman, M. (1990). Some dubious premises in research and theory on racial differences: Scientific, social, and ethical issues. *American Psychologist, 45*(12), 1297.

Index

About the Author

KEVIN O. COKLEY, PhD, is a Professor of Counseling Psychology and African and African Diaspora Studies at the University of Texas at Austin. He received his bachelor's degree in psychology from Wake Forest University, his master's degree in counselor education from the University of North Carolina at Greensboro, and his doctoral degree in counseling psychology from Georgia State University. He is the editor-in-chief of the *Journal of Black Psychology* and the director of the Institute for Urban Policy Research and Analysis (IUPRA). Dr. Cokley's research and teaching can be broadly categorized in the area of African American psychology. His research interests include the construction of racial and ethnic identities, Afrocentric psychology, academic motivation, academic self-concept, and understanding the psychological and environmental factors that impact African American student achievement. His publications have appeared in many professional journals including the *Journal of Counseling Psychology*, *Cultural Diversity and Ethnic Minority Psychology*, the *Journal of Black Psychology*, and the *Harvard Educational Review*. His 2004 article published in the *Harvard Educational Review* challenges the notion that African American students are anti-intellectual. He was elected to Fellow status in the American Psychological Association (Division 17 and 45) for his contributions to ethnic minority psychology and counseling psychology. He is the recipient of the 2014 University of Texas System Regents' Outstanding Teaching Award, the 2008 "10 Rising Stars of the Academy" award by *Diverse Issues in Higher Education*, and the 2007 Association of Black Psychologists' Scholarship Award.

About the Series

The books in this series, Practical and Applied Psychology, address topics immediately relevant to issues in human psychology, behavior, and emotion. Topics have spanned a wide range, from the psychology of black boys and adolescents, to the sexual enslavement of girls and women worldwide, and living in an environmentally traumatized world.

About the Series Editor

Judy Kuriansky, PhD, is a licensed clinical psychologist, adjunct faculty in the Department of Clinical Psychology at Columbia University Teachers College, and also the Department of Psychiatry at Columbia University College of Physicians and Surgeons. Kuriansky is a United Nations representative for the International Association of Applied Psychology and for the World Council for Psychotherapy. She is also a Visiting Professor at the Peking University Health Sciences Center, a Fellow of the American Psychological Association, Founder of the APA Media Psychology Division, and a widely known journalist for CBS, CNBC, Lifetime, and A&E, as well as a regular weekly columnist for the *New York Daily News*. She has also been a syndicated radio talk show host for more than 20 years.